# One Heart Beats for Two

C. J. Herak

Copyright © 2023 C. J. Herak
All rights reserved
First Edition

PAGE PUBLISHING
Conneaut Lake, PA

First originally published by Page Publishing 2023

ISBN 979-8-88960-484-6 (pbk)
ISBN 979-8-88960-518-8 (digital)

Printed in the United States of America

For Jillian

First and foremost, to my beloved wife, who without helping this computer idiot, I couldn't have written this story. To good friends, Lisa Lazarczyk, Mary Beth, and Tom Meros, whose experience and continual support allowed me to write this story from idea to completion.

# Chapter 1

Winston Thayer III, known as *Chip* to all that knew him, was walking down the Jetway after returning from another of his frequent business trips and was speaking loudly over his cell phone. The noise of jet engines out on the concourse and the excitement that buzzes around the airport prevented him from keeping his phone call private.

Chip was angry and was speaking even louder than what was necessary, gathering looks as he hurried past people, bumping into a small child as he brushed past. The child's mother seeing this, barked at Chip who ignored the mother's yelping as he continued on. Speaking into the phone, he said, "I'm heading into the office as soon as I get my luggage. I sure as hell hope my driver is waiting for me because when I get down to the office, I want to find out what the hell has been going on while I've been away. The last thing I needed were continual phone calls for trivial problems, while I was handling a much larger issue in California! I should be there in less than an hour, and I want everyone in the large conference room when I get there. If anyone can't be there, tell them not to show up tomorrow!"

Hanging up, he then thought about tonight. Chip had told his wife he wasn't arriving home until late in the day, and as his mind raced, he thought of the excuse he was going to give her for arriving home late tonight. Chip wanted to return to his favorite watering hole. Last week at the bar, he spotted a young woman who really caught his eye. She was with another but much older woman, and because of this, Chip felt he couldn't approach her. He also noticed that the young woman was checking him out as well. He was thinking and hoping she would be there again tonight, without the older woman so he would have the opportunity to make a play and like a great white shark captures his prey.

*****

Staring in the bathroom mirror of the hotel room where he spent the night, Chip looked closely at himself. Looking somewhat pale and feeling tired and weak, he rubbed his chest, where he had been experiencing some pain for several weeks. Looking up higher in the mirror, he could now see the young woman he'd spent the night with. She was still asleep and was naked with her back to Chip. He smiled as he again looked at himself in the mirror, suddenly feeling a pain in his chest. The pain had occurred on and off for several weeks. He wondered if his fatigued looks had anything to do with the chest pain he'd been experiencing. Chip then looked in the mirror and with a sly smile said to himself, "I can see it now, corporate executive found dead in a hotel room with an unknown naked female." *Christ*, he thought, *Candace probably wouldn't even throw me a funeral. She'd just want my body stuffed in a can and put on the curb for Monday's garbage pickup. If Candace did have a funeral, she'd probably show up with some young guy on her arm.*

*I better get this chest pain checked out*, he thought. *It's gotten worse and has happened with ever more frequency.* As Chip rubbed his chest, the woman asleep in bed turned, giving him a full-frontal look of her. He again smiled as he thought about the previous evening. Chip had met her in the hotel bar, and they proceeded to have several drinks together, but come morning, he couldn't even remember her name. Around 9:00 p.m., he excused himself and left the bar area to phone home. Candace answered, and he proceeded to lay down lie number 10,000+ on her. He said he had quite a bit to drink and decided to get a hotel room. Candace didn't argue. She could have easily come to pick him up, but she already knew the truth. This had been a reoccurring theme during their entire lousy marriage. She no longer cared but pretended to.

"I think that's a smart idea, Chip. I'll see you in the morning."

# ONE HEART BEATS FOR TWO

They hung up the phone, and Chip returned to his soon-to-be conquest back in the bar. What Chip Thayer didn't know was Candace didn't waste any time making a phone call of her own.

*****

The next morning on the other side of town, Robert (Bo) and Linda Shott were finishing their oatmeal breakfast. Simple, yet filling. They were excited as this was a rare day when both of them were off work at the same time. Both of them worked as frequently as they could as neither of them made much money, and anything they could bring in could do nothing but help. Their plans after breakfast were to take the bus over to the park, where there were walking trails. It was to be a beautiful day weather-wise, and they could enjoy each other's company to its fullest. As they stood up, Bo became dizzy. Linda didn't notice this as she was taking their breakfast bowls to the kitchen sink. Bo quietly walked into the bathroom. He was waiting for the piercing pain that he experienced after each of these dizzy spells. He hadn't mentioned any of this to Linda. The last thing he wanted to do was worry her. He also hated the idea of going to the doctor. Anytime they needed health care, it just brought on more embarrassment.

Neither of them had health insurance from their respective places of employment, and whenever they sought a doctor visit, they'd have to go over to the billing department and seek financial assistance to help pay the bill. Bo found this even more painful than the physical pain he'd been experiencing. Not being able to provide for his wife always brought him sadness. Looking into his bathroom mirror, he reached into his pocket and pulled out his lucky silver John F. Kennedy half-dollar piece. Looking at it, he wondered, *When would that luck come?* Just then, the piercing pain came to him, dropping him to one knee. After the pain somewhat subsided, he walked into the kitchen, where Linda was finishing the morning dishes. "Sweetie," he said, "do you mind if we just stay home today? I'm not feeling too well."

# Chapter 2

Candace Thayer looked at her watch and was thinking that she should be at her tennis lesson with that young, new hunk of an instructor at the club, but she realized that even with the lack of love she has for her husband, this is where she should be. She hated herself for stooping to the level of her husband, but it couldn't be helped. Chip always knew how to push her buttons, both good and bad. This loveless marriage was not due to the lack of trying on her part. She fell for Chip from the first day she saw him. They had known each other since they were kids, their parents being friends from the country club they belonged to. He was now the new kid in eleventh grade at C. J. Neff High School. Many of the other students had known him and his reputation. He may have gone to a prestigious private school, but they all grew up in the same community. Candace chased him from the start and after many pursuits got her man. He was pursued by many girls, and he accommodated all that he could, even after he and Candace became a couple.

Although it bothered her, she kept her pain inside; after all, Chip would become the class homecoming king, the "most attractive boy" in the school survey, and an all-conference lacrosse player. Who wouldn't want to get close to him? She wasn't too bad herself. She was voted the "most envied girl" in the same school survey and was a pretty decent volleyball player. Although envied, her close friends didn't understand why she played into Chip's hands. She had and continued to turn a blind eye to his dalliances.

Through the years, Chip at most was a good provider, allowing Candace to do pretty much whatever she pleased. They had two daughters, Amy, age 25 and already a successful fashion designer living in New York City, and younger daughter, Elizabeth (*who everyone calls* Betsy), nineteen and a second-year student at Capital University.

*What's taking so long?* she thought. *Where's the doctor to let her know what's going on?*

At this point, she hadn't realized how serious Chip's condition was. Candace glanced across the room, spotting another woman seated by herself with a deep look of despair on her face.

*****

Linda was seated alone, deep in her thoughts about the health problem her husband had been suffering from for the past year or so. *How could I go on if this is serious?* she thought.

Bo was everything in life to her. Neither were popular in school. As a matter of fact, most other kids never had anything to do with them and often made fun of them. It was no wonder they would eventually find each other, two discarded souls who lived similar lives. They became attracted to each other from the day they met. Both grew up in the poorest section of the city. Although raised in the same area, it being quite large, they never knew each other until meeting in tenth grade after attending different junior high schools.

*Please, God,* she thought, *Bo's all I have. We've never had much except each other. Please help us through this.*

Linda never gave a second thought about how long she'd been waiting or how long she would have to wait, as long as her Bo came out of this okay.

# Chapter 3

*It was time to get a cigarette,* Candace thought, so she went to the smoking area just outside the building. It was a habit that she had wanted to get past, but now wasn't the time. The air outside was crisp, but it felt good. It was autumn, and other than being inside for her tennis lessons, she much preferred being outside, enjoying golf, her horses, or just going for long walks. The emptiness of her marriage contributed to her independence, and being outside gave her freedom. After her smoke, she went back to the waiting area, this time making eye contact with the other lone woman. Both gave each other a sympathetic grin, although Candace measured the other woman as being somewhat beneath her.

After taking her seat back on the uncomfortable sofa and grabbing a magazine, she mindlessly started turning the pages when she heard a female voice ask her, "Do you mind if I sit with you?"

Candace looked up and, with Linda standing there, said, "Sure."

She really didn't want company, especially with this "shabby"-looking woman, but what the hell.

Linda began, "This sure is nerve-racking, this waiting."

Candace nodded. "Yes, where are these doctors, and when are they going to fill us in on what's going on?"

Linda then asked, "What brings you here?"

Candace replied, "It's my husband. He has something going on with his heart, and I thought this was just going to be a routine exploratory thing. But my god, it's been over four hours since they wheeled him in." Candace then asked, more out of courtesy than really having real concern, "What about you?"

Linda replied, "My husband's been dealing with diabetes since he was a child, and in the past year, it's really gotten out of control.

His numbers are all over the place, and they can't seem to control it. It's caused quite a bit of liver and kidney damage. I hope everything's okay." Then looking away, she said, "He's all I have in life."

At this point, Candace felt for the woman seated by her and asked, "Want to get some coffee?" Linda nodded. Linda wiped away the tears she had been shedding. They stood up and started walking to the coffee kiosk down the hall.

The coffee bar was quite busy. Linda, noticing the prices on the board, began embarrassingly scrounging through her purse for loose change. Candace took notice and thought, *Wow, this poor creature can't even afford a cup of coffee*. Turning to Linda with a soft grin, she said, "Coffee was my idea, and it will be my treat."

Linda's eyes widened, and for the first time all day, she felt good, thanking Candace almost to the point of annoyance. Candace thought, *This poor creature must be the loneliest person in the world.*

Walking back to the waiting area, Candace drank her double light mocha latte, and Linda held her cup of black coffee with both hands, grateful for a most cherished gift; the women began opening up to each other. Linda thought she recognized the woman from some time in her past. A customer at the store she works at? Maybe from school? She asked Candace where she and her husband grew up, when and where they met, and what brought them together.

Candace thought, *What the hell, it looks as if we're going to be here for quite some time, and this woman appears harmless enough.* Maybe a little conversation would be what they both needed.

Sitting back down, Candace went on to explain they had met as children, as their parents being long time friends, and they had spent time together as small children. But as they entered their pre-teens, then early teens, they had seen each other less and less, almost to the point of no longer knowing each other. Connecting again in their junior year. Chip was a new student who had transferred from a private school (*actually expelled*). They met again through various friends and started dating. After graduation, he attended Yale, and she was shipped out to a boarding school outside London (*London, yes; boarding school, no*). After graduating from Yale, Chip returned home (*she returned home the previous year*); he went to work at his father's commercial development company while she lived with her parents. They reconnected, continued dating, and were married shortly afterward. They have two daughters, now aged twenty-five and nineteen. Much of the filler she left out was more from embarrassment than time.

Linda then commented, "You must really love each other. You have two daughters, and your husband is successful." Candace just turned away and replied while shrugging her shoulders, "I suppose so." To this, Linda gave her a confused look.

Linda then began. She met Bob in the tenth grade. Both were loners, and they eventually met in the hallway after some girls had given Linda a hard time about her ratty-looking clothes and being something of a "twit." These same girls, for some reason, had dumped one of the large hallway garbage cans right in front of her locker. Bob, who was walking by, noticed Linda on the ground picking up the trash as the group of girls walked away laughing. He stopped and asked her if he could help. When she looked up, he noticed her eyes, red and watering, filled with hurt. He knew he had met his kindred spirit as he experienced much of the same from his peers.

Soon, Bob and Linda became very close friends. He would stop by her locker, and they would eventually start walking home together, because as they found out, both of them had lived in the same area, just a mile or so apart. They began to spend much of their time together. It was about this time when Bob started calling her *sweetie*. Shortly after high school, they both went to work, as college was not in either of their futures, and Bob's attempt to join the army was denied because of his diabetes. They married at nineteen.

As Linda was winding down, Bo's doctor came out. He took Linda aside to speak with her. Candace watched as they walked to a private area, and as they did, Candace started to get lost in her own thoughts.

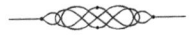

# Chapter 4

Candace was returning and getting books from her locker when her friend Mary Beth came to her and said, "Did you see the new boy that just transferred in from another school? My god, is he hot!"

As Candace started to respond, down the hall came the new boy. He was walking by himself, with a strut of confidence. Candace recognized him immediately, and as her heart began to pound, she calmly turned to her friend, saying, "Oh, that's Chip Thayer. I've known him and his parents for years."

Closing her locker and walking toward her next class, Mary Beth stared at Chip until he turned the corner at the end of the hall; Candace exhaled deeply and thought to herself, *Now is the time to get that rascal.*

Earlier in the day, some of the boys from school surrounded Chip during a study hall and asked him what school he'd transferred in from. As Chip was telling them why he was expelled, the other boys looked at him in a reserved manner. Chip went on to say that as a 3rd year man, it was his duty to haze the incoming freshmen. Previously he'd been called down several times to the headmaster's office for this, where Chip had been forewarned by the headmaster that if this continued, suspension or worse was in his future. Chip didn't care. No matter what he did, his parents wouldn't throw him to the wolves. Chip ignored the headmaster's warning.

A week later, Chip was again called down to the headmaster's office. This time a police officer was there—for what reason, Chip didn't know. What Chip did know was that one freshman boy, who Chip harassed several times, again went down to file a complaint against Chip. When Chip got word of this, he looked for the kid and gave him a rather severe beating. Chip had figured that this was the reason that he'd been called down.

As Chip entered the office, the headmaster told him to take a seat. "Your parents should be here shortly, and I want them to also hear what I have to say."

*****

Chip and his parents, now leaving the headmaster's office, exited the building. Winston Thayer II turned to his son and said, "Well, you just screwed yourself from the finest private school education in the state. You'd better cooperate at your new school because after that, it's military school. Don't test me any further, young man!"

*****

The siren from an approaching ambulance shook Candace back to her present surroundings. She looked around and, noticing Linda was still speaking with the doctor, decided to go outside for a smoke. Lighting her cigarette, she again began to drift back.

*****

Seated in the living room of her parent's home, her parents stood in front of her, Chip sat across from her, and his parents stood in front of him, as if the four adults were blocking Chip from getting near Candace. Unfortunately for all of them, Chip had already gotten more than close with Candace. The parents decided what the future had in store for the two of them.

Candace's mother then turned to her and said, "We'll be sending you to relatives outside London. You'll have the baby there."

Then Chip's father turned to him, firmly telling him, "You'll be going to Yale. I've arranged for you to be enrolled this coming fall. You'd better take college more seriously than high school if you want to be part of my company."

Candace's father then turned to the elder Chip and, with a demanding tone, asked, "Then what after graduation? I expect Chip to do the right thing."

Thayer turned to his son, saying so all could hear, "Yes, Chip will then do right by Candace and become the proper father to the child." Chip turned his head, not trying to hold his disdain, while Candace smiled, until she saw the look on Chip's face.

*****

As Candace was lost in her thoughts, her cigarette tickled her fingers. Candace dropped the remnants of the cigarette and put the two burnt fingers to her lips and quickly walked back inside the hospital. Upon entering, she walked toward the women's bathroom to run cool water over her two slightly burnt fingers, chuckling to herself. *That damn Chip, every time I think of him, something bad happens to me.* Of course, at this moment, she didn't know how bad Chip was.

Walking back to the waiting area, her mood became lighter. Linda was nowhere to be seen, so she sat back down. Being that she'd already scrolled through the magazines in the waiting area, she again drifted off to times past. This time, they were small children.

# Chapter 5

## *Flashback*

It was a very warm Sunday, and many families were taking advantage of the outdoor pool at Bushmill Country Club. Charlene Thayer was lying on a chaise while her son Winston, known to the family and relatives as *Chip*, was nearby at the kiddie pool. Seated next to her was her best friend Jayne Walters. They had met a few years earlier at the club and became fast friends. Their husbands had known each other since college, pledging to the same fraternity (*the most exclusive fraternity on campus*). After graduation, Mike Walters went to law school, becoming a successful corporate lawyer. Mike and Jayne had two children, Candace, who was six, and Brian, four. Jayne loved bringing the kids to the club to go swimming and being involved in other activities that this prestigious country club offered, as this would make for a quiet evening because generally soon after dinner, the two kids would be exhausted and wouldn't complain about going to bed.

Not out of sight, but away from their mothers' attention, Chip was teasing Candace. Initially she didn't mind, thinking it was his way of showing that he liked her. He would tug at her two-piece swimsuit, and when she went underwater, he would playfully push her head deeper into the water. Brian was watching this and was becoming scared for his sister.

Little Brian told Chip, "Stop pushing my sister."

"Shut up punk," Chip responded. Chip, obviously now trying to anger Brian, pushed Candace's head underwater for a longer period, and Brian rushed over, trying to pull Chip's arm away. Chip swatted Brian away like a fly, but it gave Candace time to come up for air. She was choking and began to cry. Both mothers then came to the kiddie pool, Jayne trying to keep peace but obviously upset and telling her kids, "Chip didn't mean anything. He was only playing."

Charlene grabbed Chip by the arm and pulled him out of the water. "If you can't play nice, you can't play at all! Time to go home." Charlene apologized to Jayne as they went their separate ways.

Candace's thoughts then moved forward to a few years later. October 26 was Brian's thirteenth birthday, and his parents were throwing him a "happy teenage birthday party," just as they did for Candace two years before. Brian was excited but a bit nervous. His parents invited friends and members of the club and, of course, all the kids that Brian ran around with. There was one girl, in particular, that he hoped would come. Her name was Lora, and Brian was crazy about her. He had crushes on girls before, but this one was different. Every time he saw her at school or spoke with her, his insides felt like "butterflies." His sister and his friends knew he liked Lora, but he didn't tell anyone about those "funny feelings" that he felt inside. Brian wanted to look good at the event. If Lora did show up, this would be the day he was going to tell her how much he did like her.

At the same time, over at the Thayer home, Teddy and Char were getting dressed to go to the party. Sure, it was a party for a young kid, but the adults always turned it into a party of their own. Let the kids have fun, with the adults carrying the good time into the late evening hours. Teddy, giggling, turned to Char and said sarcastically, "I bet Chip is excited about this."

Chip was now fifteen, and going to a "kiddie party," as Chip called it, was not his idea of fun. Char said, "Yeah, he isn't too thrilled about it, but Candace will be there, so he'll have someone of his age to hang with." With this, Char yelled, "C'mon, Chip, time to go!"

Turning to leave his bedroom, Chip in anger turned and fired a football that he had been soft tossing to himself at the pillow on his bed. "Happy birthday, you little shit, that's for you."

The party was in full swing; the gifts had been opened, one being a volleyball set. The kids set it up in an area of the vast backyard and were heavily into a game. Brian found himself on one team, and Lora was on the other. He had trouble following the ball and following Lora as she moved about on the other side of the net; in fact, when the game point was spiked, it hit him on the head, bouncing off as he never saw it coming. Brian winced and put his hand to his forehead as the winning team jumped for joy. Brian had been a little stunned and more embarrassed by this, but it turned into a blessing as Lora came to see if he was okay.

"Are you hurt?" he heard her ask. Looking up, he suddenly felt perfect.

"Yeah, I'm good. Nice game."

She smiled, and they began to walk away from the volleyball area in small talk.

At the same time, Chip was sulking around. There was not one soul his age other than Candace, and she was busy playing "hostess assistant" for her mother. Candace adored her brother and wanted to make his party a success. She bumped into Chip several times, and although she wanted to spend time with him (she really was attracted to him), her priorities right now were about Brian.

She told Chip, "Just be patient. We can spend some time together a little later."

Sunset was falling in, and many of the guests had started to leave. Several of the adults would remain to carry the party into the late evening, but now many of them along with their kids and friends of Brian began to leave. Brian was saying *thank you* to his friends and their parents as they were leaving, and at this time, Chip noticed Lora standing by herself. He thought, *Wow, young but very cute.* Chip went over to her and said hello. Lora was starstruck by this handsome older boy and quickly smiled and said *hello* back. Away in the distance, as he was saying *goodbye* to the others, Brian noticed that Chip was talking to Lora; he became both angry and nervous at the same time. After the goodbyes, Brian quickly walked over to where the two were talking.

Chip smirked at Brian and coyly said to Lora, "It was nice talking to you. Hope to see you again sometime."

Lora responded, "Yes, it was nice meeting you."

Chip, with extreme cockiness, sauntered away.

Brian said, "What did that jackass want?"

Lora, shocked at Brian's sudden showing of anger, responded, "He was very nice. Why are you so upset?"

Brian retorted, "Cuz he's an arrogant ass. I don't like him. I've never liked him!"

Now taken aback, Lora said, "Well, I had better get going."

Brian quickly replied, "Can I walk you?"

Lora replied, "That's okay. I called my mother, and she'll be picking me up in front of the house."

Brian responded, "I'll wait with you until she gets here."

"That's okay. She should be here any second. Well, happy birthday, Brian."

He wanted to kiss her; he even took one short step toward her, when she spun away and left. Brian stood there wondering what had happened, and the more he thought, the angrier he got. Looking around, he was alone. He could see the adults inside the house laughing and drinking away. His party now over and feeling miserable, Brian spun around, and spotting the new volleyball that not too long ago he along with his friends and the girl of his dreams were happily laughing and playing with, he grabbed the ball and punted it with all his might, sending it flying over the family privacy fence down into the ravine below. As he walked back to the house, his head down, he thought, *How in the hell can Candace like that asshole even a little bit.* In the back of his mind, quickly coming to the front of his mind, he wondered if another girl had just fallen for Chip also.

# Chapter 6

Chip Thayer was club champion at Bushmill Country Club for three years running. He was proud of his golf game, and he knew the other members were jealous. It wasn't jealousy; the other members disliked him for being cocky and smug and an unscrupulous businessman. He was the same with the ladies. On the golf course, he also ruled. When playing with other members of the club, there were always side bets on the outcome. Chip would love to throw away a few holes, then get his opponent to raise the bet (they were as greedy as him), then take them to the cleaners on the back nine. This strategy worked time and time again, and Chip would gloat every time he won. A few of the members also knew that Chip was involved with a few of the female members—at least two being married. The men who knew despised Chip for this but refrained from saying anything—some of them had skeletons in their own closets. It was well known around the club that Chip Thayer was a rat on the golf course, in the business world and in social circles.

# Chapter 7

Candace now looked up after coming out of her deep introspection. Linda was being walked back out to the waiting area by one of the doctors. She was visibly shaken. Candace, to her own surprise was concerned for her newfound acquaintance. Linda sat down, and after blowing her nose with a tissue, Candace asked her what news they brought her.

Linda replied, "Bob has taken a turn for the worse. They let me see him briefly, and I'm not sure if he even knew I was there. They had a tube down his throat, and he was connected to different machines." After a couple of minutes of silence, Linda said, "I'm going to the chapel. If anyone comes out looking for me, please tell them I'm there."

Candace assured her that she would. As Linda stood to leave, she gave Candace a small grin. "I hope you get some good news about your husband soon. It's really tough sitting here not knowing."

Linda then walked away. Candace just sat and thought, *How could this poor thing even think about my problems when it was obvious that her problems are so much worse?* Or so she thought.

Linda walked into the chapel, and as so often in her life, she was all alone. She lit a candle and sat in a pew in the second row. She had a small talk with God and began to reminisce. She started thinking again about the day Bo told her that he wanted to join the army. They were just about to graduate from high school, and he wanted to enlist. As they walked home from school, she kind of lost her ability to listen as Bo rambled on about the army, then hopefully community college on the G.I. Bill after that. All Linda could think was Bo going somewhere, meeting someone else, and her losing him.

It was here that she refocused on what Bo was saying. "I think we should get married before I go. Then after basic training, we could find a small place not too far from my base. Maybe you could find a job, and I could spend whatever liberty I get with you. At least we'll still be close to one another, and seeing you on occasion would be better than never seeing you."

Her mind was now racing, and she thought, *How could we afford even a small place. What if I can't find a job?*

On and on she thought until she was interrupted by Bo. "Sweetie, hello? Can you hear me?"

Linda giggled and said, "Wow, Bo, those are some plans. I mean, you really want to marry me? But we're so young." She loved it whenever he called her *sweetie*; she thought it was the nicest thing anyone ever said to her.

Bo then stopped walking, took her by both arms, and said, "Linda, I love you. You're my best friend, and the only time I'm honestly happy is when I'm with you."

As they hugged, a car passed them with a group of kids from high school. Not slowing down, someone from the car yelled, "You two losers deserve each other!"

They ignored the taunts and continued walking down the street. Bo in his excitement about the army continued speaking, "Sweetie, things will be great in the army. I can learn a trade…"

She then heard someone come into the chapel, shaking her from her thoughts.

# Chapter 8

Sitting alone, Candace thought this might be a good time to grab another smoke. She was wondering if Betsy would make it to the hospital to see her dad and keep her company. Candace also thought that maybe she should call her older daughter, Amy, who lived and worked in New York City but decided to wait until she heard something more concrete about what was going on with her husband. It was still midafternoon, so Betsy was still in class. Candace knew that Betsy wasn't crazy about her smoking, so she thought, *I'll grab a smoke while I have the chance.*

Candace then thought about Brian. Should I call him? They were always close, and although he was the younger of the two, she leaned on him as if he was the elder of them. Brian never liked Chip, and he could never understand what she saw in "that arrogant asshole," but he was always there for her. Candace thought to herself, *maybe I'll wait on calling Brian.*

As she stood, a doctor came out and said, "Mrs. Thayer, would you come with me." Away they went, with the doctor speaking to her as they walked.

*****

Linda thought it was time to go back to the waiting area, *Maybe Candace was still sitting by herself,* and as lonely as that might be, Linda felt like she needed to be by her—for both of their sakes. After getting back to the waiting area, Candace wasn't there. Linda stood just looking around. As people walked by, all involved in their own worlds and thoughts, no one had time for this person standing like a statue. Linda, looking both to her left and then right and again feeling alone, made her way over to the area where she'd been sitting. She reached for a magazine and sat down. Not opening the magazine, she just stared straight ahead.

Shortly after, Candace came back to the waiting area. Her eyes were glassy, but she hadn't been crying. Linda thought that Candace looked stunned, as if she'd been told some devastating news. Linda was just about to ask Candace what had occurred when Candace said, "His hearts not working very well, and as she began to choke up, while having a confused look on her face, "Chip's doctor said that if things don't turn around in the next few hours, they may have to look at a heart transplant!"

With this, Candace fell hard back onto her chair. Linda quickly came to her, going onto one knee and grabbing Candace's hand, as Candace tried to speak but with no words coming from her mouth. Linda, dipping her head, said a little prayer in silence.

Candace looked up, and while staring straight ahead said, "I better call my daughter in New York and have her come see her father." As she said this, Betsy, her younger daughter, came walking down the hall.

Candace stood and Betsy, seeing the look on her mother's face, approached her apprehensively. "Mom, are you all right? How's Dad?"

Candace said, "Your father's not doing too well and he may need a heart transplant."

Betsy was stunned, too stunned even to shed a tear. She asked her mother, "When will we know?"

Her mother replied, "In the next couple of hours. I'm going to give your sister a call and see if she can come."

As Candace walked away to call, she turned back to Betsy, "If Amy can catch a flight, would you be able to pick her up at the airport?"

Betsy, now trying to act strong, said, "Sure, Mom."

Betsy remained standing as she watched her mother slowly walk away. Betsy then turned toward Linda, where she and Betsy both remained silent. Candace returned a short time later and told the two standing women, "Amy's line was busy. I'll try again in a few minutes."

The three women sat down. Candace, coming to herself again, said, "Betsy, this is Linda. Her husband is also in here."

Betsy, who was the kinder of Candace's two girls, smiled and extended her hand to Linda. Shaking Linda's hand, Betsy noticed that it was very rough. *Obviously whoever this woman was, she worked hard with her hands.*

Linda said, "Very nice to meet you." Turning to Candace, she said, "Your daughter is very pretty."

Betsy lowered her head in embarrassment.

Candace, again in somewhat of a daze, stood up and said, "I'm going to call Amy."

She walked outside to the smoking area, lit a cigarette, pulled out her cell phone, and started to dial.

# Chapter 9

The office of Siebert Fashions was a busy place where upscale women's attire was designed for upscale women. Started by one woman and growing into a fashion powerhouse successful beyond the founder's wildest dreams, Amy Thayer was a much sought-after fashion designer and was a close friend of the owners' daughter while in college. Amy went to work at Siebert Fashion, after being courted by over a half dozen other fashion companies, and began working there shortly after graduation. Amy really enjoyed her career and had decided from a young age that she never wanted to be reliant on any man to secure her future, as she saw the torment her mother went through while she was growing up. Her mother was hoping that she would take a job closer to home, but as Amy told her, "If you want to make it in fashion, it was either New York or Los Angeles." Either way, the last place she wanted was to go was home. At about the age of ten was when she found out that her mother had become pregnant with her just as she was graduating from high school, and she never really felt much love from her father—as if it was her fault that her mother had become pregnant.

"No way," she would always say to herself, "I'm not going to get myself into the same mess my mother did."

Amy wasn't a "man-hater." In fact, she had her share of boyfriends and sexual experiences herself, but on her terms, and she always made certain that all precautions were to be taken to prevent an unwanted pregnancy. If the partner she was with didn't agree, then he needed to go elsewhere to find pleasure.

Amy was very busy working on some type of issue with a new line of women's dresses when her secretary called her saying that she had an important call. Not wanting to break her concentration, she became annoyed at the interruption but took the call anyway. "This is Amy Thayer," she said into the phone.

"Hello Amy, it's Mom."

Amy, with a quick roll of her eyes in disdain, then quickly shaking it off, said, "Hi, Mom, what's up? I'm pretty busy."

Candace started to tell her on the other end of the phone what was going on, and Amy's look went from disdain, to annoyance, then to concern. Amy felt for her mother more than she did for her scoundrel of a father and, as she continued to listen, interrupted her mother, "Okay, let me see if I can get a flight out tonight, and I'll get back to you."

After a bit of small talk, Amy hung up the phone. *Damn it*, she thought, *I really don't have time for this now*. She called to her secretary, "Janice, see if you can find me a flight to Cleveland tonight. I have to get there right away."

# Chapter 10

While on the flight, Amy started thinking about her parents when she was a young child. She knew they argued quite a bit. Her parents thought Amy wouldn't understand their arguments, but she was smart, street-smart beyond her years. She had an inkling that her "loving" father was messing around with other women. While attending events at their private club, she noticed her father getting "too close" with a variety of women, and she knew this made her mother furious. She also knew this is what caused her mother to drink more than she felt was right. Amy was becoming angry, and her anger continued to rise as she thought of her parents and the phony façade they "played up" socially. Being wealthy and popular, they portrayed the "happy couple." Amy vowed she would never let her life be dictated by a man, then, suddenly shocked, asked herself, "Will I ever be able to fall in love?" She then cursed her parents under her breath, "Fuck. Thanks, Mom and Dad. Not only did you give me a shitty childhood. It has me all messed up as an adult."

# Chapter 11

Driving back from the airport, Betsy and Amy chatted about what's been going on in their lives. Betsy was somewhat shocked at her sister's language and attitude in general. Betsy always looked up to her older sister. Betsy was always impressed on how independent Amy was, never hesitant on going her own way, to do what she wanted to do, and never being pressured by her parents or friends into doing something that she didn't want to do or participate in. If there was some other direction she wanted to go, she would just say, "see ya later," and go her own way. She liked sports, but individual sports, and she became a very adept golfer and tennis player. She didn't compete in high school, because even those activities involved being a part of a team. Instead, she played at the country club her family were members of, and she would often become club champion in both sports in her age bracket. Since graduating from school and getting deeply involved in her career, the days of competitive golf and tennis have passed, as she was smart enough to realize that although very good at golf and tennis, she wasn't good enough to make a living at it. She immersed herself into her career, and she felt she was "very good at it."

As Betsy began to update Amy on what's been going on with her life during her second year of college, Amy only partially listened. Amy loved her younger sister but at times became annoyed at her sister's light personality and the ability to keep control, never showing anger or a spoiled demeanor, both something that Amy had a difficult time hiding. Amy knew her father preferred Betsy, and unlike herself, Betsy wasn't an "unfortunate accident." At times Amy held Betsy in contempt for this, but that faded as Amy became more aware that it wasn't Betsy's fault that she wasn't born first.

During the conversation, Amy brought up dating, then asked Betsy, "So do you have a boyfriend or what?"

Betsy responded, "No, I go out with a couple of boys, but nothing serious. It seems there are very few boyfriend/girlfriend relationships in the group I hang around with. We do most things as a group." Betsy didn't offer that she wouldn't mind having a steady boyfriend, but at the time it just wasn't happening.

Before Betsy could finish her thought, Amy said, "You're better off, especially at your age. So tell me, little sister, are you still a virgin?"

The comment really startled her. Betsy really didn't want to give her the real answer—yes, she was. Betsy just responded in a joking manner, "I'm sorry, big sister, my personal life is personal."

Amy just responded with a sarcastic chuckle, "Remember (*as Amy spoke, she lit a cigarette*) don't ever become dependent on men. It can only lead to a life of misery. After all, look at Mom."

Betsy, somewhat alarmed, said, "When did you start smoking?"

Amy responded, "Grow up, little sister. My job is stressful, and I can't keep a bottle of vodka on my desk."

Betsy was taken aback, not only by her sister's smoking but also by her icy insight into her parents' relationship. Betsy knew that her parents' relationship never appeared to be overly loving, but she never looked at her mother as a hostage. Betsy also knew that she was closer to her father than Amy was, and it wasn't until the girls were old enough to put it all together to realize that the conception of Amy and birth came before a wedding. As she was driving, her mind was racing. Amy was talking about something, but Betsy didn't hear what she was saying. At that moment, it struck Betsy, she knew that she was her father's little girl, much more so than Amy. Both girls were close with their mother, although Amy almost seemed as much a friend to her mother as well as a daughter. This never bothered Betsy, she just assumed that being the firstborn, that's the way it was.

But this sudden revelation of hers caused her to swerve the car slightly. *Dad blames Amy for altering his life*, she thought. *It was her fault for being born!*

Amy yelled out, "Hey! Pay attention!"

Betsy, regaining her composure, quickly apologized, "Sorry about that."

"Christ," Amy said, "let's get to Mom and the old man in one piece!"

Betsy again apologized, then laughed and said, "You want to know something? You sound just like Dad."

Amy responded, "Chrissake, shut up and drive."

Now she understood why Amy felt the way she did toward her father. They didn't speak for the rest of the drive to the hospital.

# Chapter 12

Walking to the waiting area of the hospital, the two girls saw their mother sitting on a small sofa next to a somewhat unkempt woman. Candace looked up as Amy and Betsy approached her. Candace stood up, embracing Amy. Candace spoke first as she wiped away a tear, "Hi, honey, I'm glad you could make it. You look lovely."

Amy, feeling a series of mixed emotions for her mother, then said, "Momma, you're looking well. How's Dad?"

Candace went on in detail describing what's been going on since early that morning. There were no new developments since Betsy had left the hospital to pick up her sister at the airport.

"When can we see him?" asked Amy.

Candace replied, "We'll have to wait until the doctor comes back out. I've seen the doctor just about every hour or so. Your sister hasn't seen your father yet either, so hopefully the next time the doctor comes out, we can go in to see him."

Amy then looked down at the pitiful woman who had been sitting next to her mother.

Candace said, "Amy, this is Linda. Her husband is in intensive care."

Linda stood to greet her new friend's firstborn daughter. With this, Amy gave a quick cold *hello*. Linda quickly sat back down, and Candace was upset about the rudeness of her elder daughter, but she didn't want to start anything now. She was just happy her two girls were now with her.

A while later, after all the updating of their lives had been completed and brief silence was the only noise to be heard, they heard footsteps. As they looked up, it was the doctor who had been coming out hour after hour. Candace introduced the doctor to the two girls with them quickly asking if they could see their father. The doctor, although somewhat hesitant, said, "Of course, for a few minutes." The four then headed down the hall to their father's room.

# Chapter 13

Sitting alone like she's been so many times in her life, Linda now began to think back at her life after she had met and then married Bo. The two of them lived upstairs above a neighborhood barbershop. The place was rather small, with one bedroom, a small but functional kitchen, a bathroom with tub and shower, and a modest living room. Even with both of them working, they could never afford their own home. At one time, that seemed to bother them, but they came to realize that no matter where they lived, as long as they were together, that's all that mattered. Other than each other, neither of them had what you would call a "best friend," and it was a rare day when either of them spent any time with an acquaintance or co-worker. When this rare event did occur, they encouraged each other to have a good time. It was unfortunate that neither of them had common friends, and it was either one of them going out while the other remained at home, and after a period of a few years, both would politely refuse to go out when asked, so as to not leave the other alone. Their love for each other was absolute. As she sat alone, Linda was thinking of Candace and her two daughters and what Linda would have given to have a child of her own.

*****

(Flashback) It was the day to visit the doctor, and Linda and Bo were very nervous. For several years, they had tried to conceive a child, but without success. Two weeks ago, they went to a fertility doctor and tests were taken, and today was the result day. Arriving at the office twenty minutes early, they were told to take a seat. Nervously they both leafed through magazine after magazine seemingly for an eternity when they heard, "Mr. and Mrs. Shott." They jumped up, almost as if they had been shocked, and followed the nurse back to the doctor's office. A rarity indeed, the doctor was already in the office going over the test results. Bob and Linda sat down, and the doctor began to speak. Apparently the problem was due to Bo's diabetic condition. It had caused some type of issue where he could not produce the "necessities" to fertilize his wife. Neither of them could comprehend the technical terms the doctor spilled out, but what they did understand was that their hope of being parents would not happen. The doctor stated that he would gather some information for them in the event they would want to try and adopt. They stood up and thanked the doctor and exited the room, both in silence.

As they walked out of the office and entered the elevator to leave the building, Bo put his arm around Linda, kissed her on the cheek, and said, "Can I buy my sweetie an ice cream?"

Linda, wiping away a tear, turned to Bo with a small grin and said, "Sure." She noticed that he also had tears in his eyes.

# Chapter 14

Standing next to their father's bed, Candace whispered to her husband, "Chip, the girls are here."

Chip had been borderline conscious, but when he heard what Candace had said, his eyes opened somewhat. He said, "Hi," in a whisper. It was unbelievable to them that the strong, dominant man they had known since they were born was now this frail-looking specimen.

All three of them leaned over and kissed him on the forehead. Just as quickly as he perked up, he fell back into semiconsciousness. They stood for a few moments then left the room. As they were heading back to the waiting area, Amy's phone buzzed. Looking at her text message, Amy said, "Chrissake, what now?" She turned to her mother and sister and said, "It's New York. There's some bullshit problem. I've got to call them."

As she walked away, it struck Candace immediately. She knew that Amy wasn't crazy about her father, but her facial expressions and vocabulary were a spot-on match to her father. In a strange sort of way, especially with what was going on, this made Candace let out a little chuckle, which surprised Betsy.

"What is it, Mom?" said Betsy, as she and Candace continued to walk to the waiting area.

"Nothing, honey." *The daughter who the father blamed for being born had become him.* Candace just shook her head.

Arriving back at the waiting area, Linda was seated alone. Linda sat at attention when they returned and asked Candace, "Any news?"

Candace just replied, "When I told him the girls were here, he briefly opened his eyes and said *hi* then fell back to sleep."

Amy was walking back in their direction with a look of annoyance on her face and said, "You'd think those assholes could handle things for ten minutes while I'm away." She began to pace, and even more so, she had taken on the persona of her father.

Candace seemed to be unaffected by her daughter's language (after all, she was her father's daughter), but Betsy, catching the uncomfortable look on the face of Linda, apologized for her sister's outburst. Linda just sheepishly nodded.

Candace excused herself, "I'm going outside for a cigarette."

With this, Amy responded, "I'll join you."

Candace, walking toward the door, didn't seem to be surprised that her elder daughter, who lived in the big city, became a smoker. She silently hoped that was the worst habit she'd had. The two headed to the exit. Betsy and Linda just sat and smiled at each other.

Betsy spoke first, "How long have you been married?"

Linda responded, "Next Tuesday, we'll be married for twenty-six years."

Betsy said, "That's quite an accomplishment! How many children do you have?"

Linda responded, almost embarrassed, "Well, we were never fortunate enough to have children."

Betsy quickly responded, "I'm sorry."

Linda just shook her head, as if to say *that's okay.*

Betsy then excused herself, saying, "Are you okay here by yourself? I'll be back in a few minutes. I need to make a phone call." Betsy then looked around to see if her mother and sister were heading back to the waiting area—they were not. Betsy then said, "I can wait until my mother and sister return."

Linda responded, "No, go right ahead. I don't mind. Maybe our doctor will be coming out soon."

Betsy then said, "I'll make it quick. I don't want you to be here alone."

Linda smiled, and Betsy walked away swiftly. As Betsy walked away, Linda started thinking about the three women that were around her. It was apparent that they had money, yet they seemed almost distant from each other, a coolness that Linda didn't understand.

As she sat alone, she adjusted her sweater and started to reminisce. It was Christmas, and Bo and she were sitting in their living room, around the small Christmas tree that they just put up the day before. The tree was from a local store, and since Christmas was just two days away, the store was practically giving them away, which was fortunate for them as it was the only way they could afford it. Bo gave Linda her Christmas present, which happened to be the sweater she was now wearing. She was so happy, and Bo kept asking her, "Are you sure you like it?" He kept saying, "I wish it was more, sweetie. I wish I could have gotten you more." And Linda kept telling him, "I love it. It's my favorite color." As the memory started to fade, Betsy returned.

# Chapter 15

Outside the hospital, both Candace and Amy were into their second cigarette. Candace was trying to explain to Amy the relationship that she and her father had. Candace was fully aware that Amy had been angry for years at her father for his ways, not only for his coldness toward her, but also the way he made his mother look foolish. Amy was street-smart at a very young age (again, a trait of her father), and she knew that he messed around with other women. Yes, her father was a very attractive man, and he didn't have to search out women—they flocked to him. Amy knew this upset her mother terribly, and as bad as it was, if he did his philandering while out of town on business (*which he probably did*), that could be tolerated. But good ole Chip Thayer made his rounds with local women, especially the women from the club. Amy had almost wished a jealous husband would beat the shit out of him, not kill him, but beat him up so other people could see the physical damage to that pretty face.

Candace said, "Look, honey, your father and I have had a difficult relationship, but he's always been a good provider, sent you and your sister to tremendous private schools, and gave you opportunities that most kids couldn't even dream of."

Amy raised her voice, "Yeah, great private *boarding* schools. He never wanted me around. Did he ever call me? No. Did he ever visit? No. The only time I spoke with him is when you called me and you'd put him on the phone, or I called you and he did the same. The only time he came to my school was either to drop me off or pick me up on a school break. I don't care about the perks we had with his financial success. I'd rather have had a dad who was poor but loved me."

Candace then hugged Amy, who was now lightly weeping. Candace said, "Honey, some people just don't know how to show love. Besides don't think your mother has been a total victim. I'll tell you this, but I don't want your sister to know. Betsy adores your father. I know he's shown more love toward her than you and me combined, but I've strayed, more than once. Whether your father knows or cares, I have no way of knowing."

With this, Amy broke the hug and, with tears on her face, smiled and said, "Good for you, Mom. You deserved happiness."

"No!" Candace shouted more loudly than she'd meant. "I've hated myself for this. Some of the men I've been with, I did just for spite. If I could take it all back, I would."

Amy then replied, "It would be nice if the old man felt the same."

"Maybe I've given your father reasons to stray?" said Candace.

"Mother, quit beating yourself up over this." Amy then smiled at her mother, gave her a hug, and said, "Let's go back inside."

# Chapter 16

When Candace and Amy returned to the waiting area, Betsy was seated next to Linda, and they were chatting, stopping and looking up as Candace and Amy returned. Candace and Amy then sat next to each other. Amy looked at Linda and couldn't help but think that this woman was beneath the three of them but began to soften as she listened to Linda talk. It was very apparent that this woman was truly in love with her husband, and they had something that her mother and father didn't. Betsy then asked Linda how the two of them met and how they ended up together. Linda proceeded to tell the story of how they met in school and became so close to each other.

"We never had much in the way of money and possessions, but Bo is the most considerate person I've ever known. He always called me *sweetie*," she said as a small grin came across her face while wiping away a tear. Now almost laughing, she said, "Sometimes I think he's forgotten my name. He never calls me *Linda*, always *sweetie*." Then becoming somber, she said, "I just don't know how I'll manage if I," she pauses, "lose him."

Amy just swallowed hard and turned away as Betsy took Linda's hand and said, "I'm sure he'll be fine."

Linda then excused herself, "Excuse me, Betsy, did you notice where the bathrooms are?"

Betsy responded, "Yes, they are around the corner, down the hall on the left."

Linda said, "Thank you," as she started to walk toward the bathroom she then turned back and said, "If the doctor comes out to speak with me, would you come and get me?"

They all either shook their head or responded *yes*. Once Linda was out of earshot, Betsy said, "That poor woman, she's all alone, and she loves her husband so much. Talking with her, she and her husband have nothing but each other. It may sound crazy, but I'd give up everything I own to find love like that."

Candace just looked away, about to burst out in tears. Amy looked at Betsy, first with a quick look of disdain, then she coolly said, "I don't know of anyone who has love like that," then with her voice softening, "I suppose with that kind of love, you really don't need anything else?"

After several minutes, the three of them were in quiet thought, and walking in their direction came Bo's doctor, at the same time Linda was returning from the bathroom. Seeing the doctor, she walked quickly to where the three ladies were seated.

The doctor then said, "Mrs. Shott, would you come with me." The doctor and Linda walked away as the three ladies watched them step into an office with a glass window.

Candace, now looking concerned, leaned forward and said, "Oh my god, this can't be good."

Betsy then sat closer to her mother, putting an arm around her. Amy then sat next to her mother on the other side, actually taking her mother's hand. The three of them couldn't hear what was being said, but they didn't need to. Linda was now crying and lowering her head. At one point, Linda looked up at the doctor and nodded. The doctor then came from being seated across and now sat next to her, putting his arm around her and handing Linda a paper. Linda quickly read it and signed the paper.

Candace now said aloud, "No, this can't be happening. It isn't fair!"

The doctor and Linda came out of the office and went back to the room where her husband was. The three women were now quietly frantic, worrying sick for their kindred friend. Candace, now standing and to the point of anger, was saying, "I'm going to ask what's going on."

Betsy then pulled her back down. "Mom, they aren't going to tell us anything."

Some minutes later, out came Linda with one of the attending nurses. Linda was crying as the nurse was asking her questions which none of them could hear. Linda just slowly shook her head no.

As the nurse turned and walked away, Candace and the two girls hurried up to Linda's side, with Candace taking Linda by both arms. "Linda, what is it? What did they tell you?"

Linda responded, "He's too far gone. They can't save him…they wanted to know…I had to sign a paper…"

As she turned for the door to leave, Betsy then said, "Linda, can I drive you home?"

Linda shook her head and said, "No, thank you. I'll take the bus. You need to be here with your mother. She and your father need your support."

Betsy became befuddled, thinking to herself, *This woman just heard the worst news of her life, and she's thinking of someone else's misfortune?*

Candace then hugged Linda and asked her, "Can I call you sometime…would you like to come over some evening…anything?"

Linda just responded, "Candace, I'll pray for your husband. I hope all goes well and he gets another chance to live a happy life. Thank you again for keeping me company, and for the coffee." With this, Linda turned and walked away.

Candace was dumbfounded, saying to herself, but out loud, "She just lost her husband, and she thanks me again for the coffee?" Turning to the girls, she said, "I've got to find out what the hell happened here."

Just then, out came Chip's doctor. As the doctor approached them, he had a strange, relieved look on his face. "Mrs. Thayer, can I speak with you in private?"

Candace replied, "Doctor, these are my two daughters Amy and Betsy, and they should hear anything you want to speak with me about."

Both girls shook hands with the doctor. There was no one else near, so the doctor pulled up a chair and started to tell what was happening, "Mrs. Thayer, we can't save your husband unless he receives a new heart." The three women all became startled. "Fortunately, we have a positive donor, and remarkably so, the donor was from this facility. Usually when a heart is donated, it would be sent to a person on a heart transplant waiting list. Being we have a donor and recipient at the same facility, we can bypass any waiting list and perform the procedure here. We do need your written permission to perform the surgery, as there's no guarantee that the procedure will be successful."

Although shocked by the news, the three women now had hope for Chip, with Candace replying, "Yes, Doctor, of course, what do I need to sign?"

"Could you follow me, please? I can give you the necessary forms, if you two ladies don't mind waiting here?"

Both girls nodded as Candace rose to follow the doctor. As they walked away, Amy stood up, telling Betsy, "I'm going to call my office and tell them I won't be back in for the rest of the week."

Betsy said, "Okay, I'll wait here for Mom."

In the doctor's office, Candace quickly went over the papers and signed them. She then asked the doctor, "Can you tell me who the donor was?"

The doctor nodded affirmatively, "Yes, the woman you've been seated with, it was her husband."

Candace, while remaining stoic, was frantic on the inside, thinking quickly to herself, *This isn't fair*. Although being grateful, she immediately started thinking about the woman who just lost everything. "Doctor, would you give me the woman's address and phone number? I...I just have to talk with her...or send her something. That poor woman."

The doctor replied, "Let's see what I can do about that, but for now, would you like to see your husband before we start the procedure? Your girls can come back with you."

The two of them walked back out to the waiting area, where Amy had returned from her phone call, smelling fresh from a smoked cigarette, which Candace felt like she could really use right now.

"What is it, Mother?" Betsy asked.

"Girls, let's go see your father before they start the surgery."

Amy, noticing the glassy look in her mother's eye said, "Mom, what is it?"

Candace replied, "I'll tell you after we see your father."

The four of them then headed back to see him. In his room, Chip was either in a coma or some type of unconsciousness. Candace asked, "Will he be strong enough to go through this?"

The doctor responded, "He's been given a presurgical sedative, so he doesn't know you're here."

The three ladies each leaned over and kissed him on the cheek; then the doctor turned to them and said, "You may want to go home and get some rest. This is going to be a long procedure."

Betsy asked, "How long, Doctor?"

"If all goes smoothly, approximately eight hours. If we run into something else, it could be considerably longer. We will be calling a backup team to be here on standby in the event we run into an unforeseen problem."

The three women nodded. Chip's doctor exited the room as the nurse turned them back toward the waiting area. Candace was the last of the three to leave Chip's room she noticed a silver coin right next to Chip's pillow. Candace thought, *What was it doing there?* She picked it up and took it with her. *What was a coin doing by his pillow? How could something like that fall out of someone's pocket?* She then cupped it in her left hand and left the room.

Now back in the waiting area, as the three of them stood there, Amy said, "What do you think, Mom, you've been here for a long time already. Do you want to go home and take a nap?"

Candace replied, "No, I want to be here in the event…it doesn't go right."

Betsy chimed in, "I'm staying also."

Amy agreed, "Okay, Mom, why don't we get some coffee."

As the three women entered the cafeteria, Betsy asked her mother, "Mom, do you want something to eat while we're here?"

Candace shook her head no. "Just coffee, you girls eat something if you're hungry."

Amy responded, "I've got to grab something. I have an upset stomach from not eating anything all day."

Betsy chimed in, "I could go for a muffin. I'm pretty hungry."

With their coffee, both girls also grabbed a muffin. Finding an empty seat, they sat down. Taking a sip of their coffee and just before biting into her muffin, Amy asked her mother, "Mom, when you came back out to the waiting area, you had a far-off look in your eye. Is there something you haven't told us?"

With this, both Amy and Betsy took a bite of their muffin and started chewing. Candace replied in disbelief, while looking straight ahead, "Yes, the heart going into your father…came from…Linda's husband."

Both girls immediately stopped chewing. Betsy covered her mouth, almost choking, as she responded, "Oh my god!"

Amy finished chewing and then said, "That poor woman."

Candace then spoke up, almost frantically, "I've got to call Linda, or go see her, something!" Then in a moment of confusion, she said, "She wished your father to get well. She knew he was going to receive her husband's heart!" She then trailed off, "She didn't even mention it." The three women then just sat there in silence.

Candace never did say anything to the two girls about the silver coin she had found.

# Chapter 17

## *Flashback*

Bo looked under the bed, on his dresser, and in the bathroom searching for his "good luck" coin. "My gosh," he said. "I hope I didn't lose that coin."

Just then, Linda came walking into the bedroom and said, "Bo, is this yours?"

Relieved, Bo took the coin as Linda reached out to him. "Whew, I was starting to panic," said Bo. Taking the coin from Linda, he said, "I've never told you, but this is my good luck coin, a 1964 John F. Kennedy silver half-dollar. My mother gave it to me when I was a little guy for my birthday. She said, 'Go buy yourself some candy.' The coin was so shiny that I never wanted to part with it, so I'd always carry it in my pocket, you know, for good luck."

Linda then asked, "Do you really think it's lucky?"

Bo responded with a smile, "I had it in my pocket the day I met you!"

# Chapter 18

The women were into their third hour of waiting as the procedure continued on, most of it in silence. Amy had softened her attitude during this time, realizing that her mother really did love her father, even if he rarely showed it.

Betsy, of course, was the closest to her father, even more so than Candace, and she was showing the most agitation on how her father was doing. "Jesus, I know they said this would take quite a while, but you'd think they could come out and give us an update."

Candace replied, "Honey, I'm sure when they know something, we'll know something."

Candace now looked up and noticed that walking in their direction was her brother Brian. The three ladies saw him all at the same time and stood to greet him, with Brian hugging his big sister first. "Candy, have you heard anything?"

Candace began to cry while she embraced Brian. "Nothing yet. I was just telling the girls that I'm sure we'll hear something when they know something."

With this, Brian went and gave Amy a hug and, with a little joke, said, "How's my New York Yankee?"

Amy chuckled and said, "Doing fine, Uncle Brian. How are you?"

Brian responded, "Never better."

With this, Candace gave Brian a quick look. *Never better? Was Brian saying this because he never liked Chip, or was he being sincere?* As quick as the thought came into her head, she let it go. Brian and she were always close, and she knew that he was there to support her, and for that, she was appreciative.

Brian now turned to Betsy. "How you doing, baby? Thanks for calling me. I knew you'd both be here for your mother, but I'm glad I could be with her also."

Betsy replied, "I'm doing well, Uncle Brian. You look good!"

Brian responded, "I'm feeling good."

Again, Candace looked at Brian and again quickly dismissed his reply. As they sat back down, Brian asked, "So what do we know."

Candace began filling Brian in on what they knew. Candace also mentioned the poor lonely woman who was with her, also waiting for information on the status of her husband's situation. "Brian, I wish you could have met her, this woman and her husband may have been more in love than any couple I've ever known. These two had nothing but each other. They had no children. They had no money, no friends, just each other, and they were completely happy! According to her, he treated her like an angel, and now she's lost him."

Brian asked, "What was the cause of his death?"

Candace replied, "The poor guy had a multitude of health problems and was suffering from liver and kidney failure. When she came out after seeing him for the last time, she was crying but came over to us to wish Chip's recovery! It was after she left that we found out it was her husband's heart that they are placing in Chip!"

Brian said, "Oh my god, that's beyond unreal. Have you gotten any information on the woman, her address or phone number? You've got to get ahold of her, and I don't know, thank her, comfort her, something."

Candace said, "I was going to go up to the desk and see if they'd give me any information."

Brian stood and said, "I'll get it," and quickly walked up to the desk with the three women watching him the entire time. They couldn't hear what was being said, but Brian was getting animated and was looking agitated. He soon returned to the three and said, "They won't tell me anything. They said I'm not an immediate family member. I then tried to explain that you three had enough to worry about. But the desk nurse only said, 'Sorry, immediate family only.'"

After hearing this, Candace stood up and walked over to the information desk and started, "Yes, I'd very much appreciate it if you'd give me the phone number and address of the woman who was seated with me much of the day. I really need to contact her."

The desk nurse replied, "I'm sorry, ma'am, that kind of information cannot be given out, unless the doctor who's performing the procedure on your husband allows it, and right now, I think he's a little busy."

Candace was in no mood and didn't have the energy to get into it with this sarcastic nurse, so she turned and walked back to the others.

Amy asked, "What'd they tell you, Mom?"

Candace replied, "The doctor is the only one who can release that information," then imitating the voice of the nurse, "and right now, I think he's a little busy." The other three let out a little chuckle.

# Chapter 19

The four of them sat in silence, as the "catching up" had been completed about an hour ago. Now into their seventh hour of waiting, which felt much longer, sitting there each one of them was in their own thoughts about Chip. Brian was thinking how this guy was always a pain in the ass to him, and if he pulled through this thing, hopefully he'd change. He didn't care if Chip still treated him like he didn't exist, but he hoped he started treating his sister better, the louse. As Brian was finishing up his thoughts, out came the doctor.

The doctor looked tired as he sat down with the four of them. Sitting back and letting out a long sigh, he proceeded to tell them how things were with Chip, "The procedure went well. Your husband's under sedation, and I'll take you back to see him. I must tell you though, the first twenty-four hours are critical. There's no way of knowing if his body will accept or reject the new heart. After you see him, which can only be for a few minutes and only through the observation window, I suggest you go home and get some rest yourselves. If something happens, we'll be sure to contact you immediately."

Betsy then said, "Doctor, can we go in and give him a kiss?"

The doctor shook his head. "Absolutely not, we can't risk him catching an infection."

With this, they all stood up. Candace pulled the doctor aside, sternly asking him, "Doctor, I must have Linda's last name, address, and phone number." Then glancing at the others, she said, "We must send her something or, at the very least, I have to call her. My god, it was her who gave the okay to have her husband's heart put into my husband! I just can't ignore that fact. You've got to give me that information!"

The doctor thought for a moment then nodded his head affirmatively. "All right, after I take you back to see your husband, I'll get you the information."

Candace replied with relief, "Thank you, Doctor, thank you for everything."

The four then walked back to see Chip.

# Chapter 20

The three women were now in the car with Betsy driving. Brian was going to meet them at their house after making a stop to pick up some food for the four of them. Amy started, "It's good to see Uncle Brian. He must really love you, Mom, because I know he hates Dad."

Candace spoke, holding the silver coin she'd found tightly in her left hand, "He doesn't hate your father."

With this, Betsy chimed in, "C'mon, Mom, we all know the history of how Dad treated Uncle Brian."

Candace admitted defeat, "Well, he didn't treat him very well when we were kids, but as we grew up, it wasn't that bad."

Amy replied, "Whatever you say, Mom."

The car became silent, and Candace was deep in her thoughts about Linda and her lost love, Bo, how he always referred to her as "sweetie." Candace thought to herself, *With all that I have, I think I'd give it all to have what she'd had.*

Arriving home, Betsy pulled the car up near the front door and shut the engine off, and they exited the car. Candace was holding in her right hand the paper with Linda's address and phone number in a vicelike grip and the silver coin in her left.

# Chapter 21

The nurses were doing their follow-up on Chip while he was in recovery, checking his vitals and oxygen levels. The man with the new heart was placed in a post-op induced coma.

Chip was having a dream during this period.

He was in a board meeting, and the discussion was getting heated over whether the company should get involved in various causes plaguing society and, as a group, consider starting a foundation of some type, making both individual and corporate donations to these causes.

Chip, speaking up, was adamant, "There's no way corporations should enter into the 'donating business.' Corporations must focus more of their efforts on building businesses. If each of you is compelled to donate your hard-earned money, feel free. In my view, this is a private thing, and I prefer to keep it that way."

The other board members looked at each other, not with surprise (as they all knew Chip was always about himself and himself alone) but with disdain. The company was doing great, and with so many people hurting in an otherwise down economy, they all felt it would be good for the community and for their bottom line. They all knew though, regardless of their joint opinions, that it was Chip who had the final word. As they got up to leave the meeting, two of the board members whispered to each other, "What a cheap bastard," one said, with the other replying, "He's not cheap, he's greedy."

*****

The nurses again checked his vitals, noticing a sudden irregularity in his heart rhythm. A call on the PA system was put out for Chip's doctor. By the time Chip's doctor arrived in the room, his vitals had returned to normal.

# Chapter 22

The four of them were now seated around the dining room table eating the food Brian brought to the house. They consumed every morsel. Candace, feeling guilty about how much she ate, didn't realize how hungry she actually was. They were talking about the way the day went and the events that led up to the heart transplant when Brian made the comment, "A new heart eh, do you think it will take?"

The various reactions were kept silent but were conflicting. Betsy thought, *Will the new heart be accepted by her father's body?* Candace thought, *Does Brian actually have concern?* It was only Amy who saw through the comment, letting out a short giggle at knowing what her uncle meant. *Will the new heart actually change this self-centered man?*

Betsy gave her older sister a quick look of disgust as Candace rose quickly to start cleaning off the table. She then asked as she carried some of the dinnerware into the kitchen, "Would anybody like some coffee?" They all answered affirmatively and took the remaining plates—clean of the food they'd just eaten into the kitchen.

# Chapter 23

The next morning, the three women were back at the hospital, waiting for the doctor to come out to hopefully take them back and see Chip. They'd been there about two hours when the doctor finally came out. The three stood up as the doctor said, "Ladies, he's coming out of the induced coma, and you can come back to see him, but let me tell you something first. It's looking very promising, but he isn't out of the woods just yet, so you can see him for a couple of minutes, but that's all. I suggest you then go home. There isn't anything we can do but show patience at this point. Of course, if anything should happen, we'll contact you immediately."

The three women followed the doctor with great anticipation to Chip's room. Even Amy was anxious to see if her father was doing well. When they arrived in the room, the three women went to one side of the bed, with Candace closest to Chip, as the doctor went to the other side. The doctor then lightly shook Chip's shoulder. Chip's eyes were closed with his head in the direction of the doctor. "Mr. Thayer, Mr. Thayer, your family's here."

Chip slowly opened his eyes, looking at the doctor; then turning toward his family, with a weak voice and smile, he looked directly at Candace and said, "Hi, sweetie."

# Chapter 24

Betsy and Amy both let out a great sigh of relief and gave each other a hug as Candace just stood in stunned silence. She immediately felt chills up and down her spine. Betsy, noticing her mother just standing and not saying anything, turned to Candace and said, "Mother, say something."

Candace shook her head up and down. "Chip, Chip, how are you feeling?"

Chip just tilted his head slightly and said, "Never better," then drifted back to sleep.

The doctor told the women, "Okay, that's it for now."

With that, Amy and Betsy exited the room, with Candace temporarily frozen. Slowly turning, she exited the room as Amy and Betsy gave each other a second hug. Candace continued walking absolutely floored about what she'd heard.

As Betsy was driving back to their home, the conversation between Amy and Betsy was nonstop, with great excitement in their voices. They were so encouraged by the status of their father; this was the happiest they'd been as a family in quite some time. Candace, seated in the back seat, was relatively quiet, responding to her daughters with one word answers.

Amy's phone rang. "This is Amy Thayer. (pause) Yes, hello. (pause) He's doing very well, thank you. Listen, I'm in the car with my mother and sister. Let me give you a call when we get back to the house. (pause) About ten minutes. (pause) Okay, talk to you soon."

Candace then asked Amy, "Anything wrong, honey?"

"No, they just need my go-ahead on a project."

With that, the three sat in silence for the remainder of the drive. A few minutes later, Betsy pulled in the driveway, and the women exited the car. As Amy walked away from the other two, she started dialing her phone. As Betsy and Candace walked to the front door of the house, Betsy took Candace's arm, stopping her mother, and asked, "Mom, what's wrong?"

Candace, looking Betsy directly in her eyes, said, "Did you hear what your father called me? He said, 'Hi, sweetie.'"

Betsy then immediately knew why her mother had the reaction that she had. "Mom, you don't think?"

Candace replied, "I don't know, honey, I just don't know."

The two of them then continued into the house. After entering the house, Betsy excused herself and left the room. Candace stood there thinking and softly saying out loud to herself, "Where did I put that coin?" She quickly moved about the dining room, looking on the table, fireplace mantle, and end tables; then she stopped and thought, *Of course*, and went into the kitchen where she found the coin next to the sink. She picked it up, held it in her left hand, and stared out the kitchen window. Betsy, coming back, saw her mother just standing there and asked, "Mom, you alright?"

Candace turned, squeezed the coin a bit tighter, and gave Betsy a small grin.

# Chapter 25

Chip had now been in the hospital for ten days, and things were looking good for him. His body fully accepted the new heart, and he'd now been awake and alert for several days. Amy went back to New York a week ago but stated she would return when her father was released from the hospital. Candace had been contemplating the best way to contact Linda. With Betsy's input, Candace decided to send Linda flowers, with a handwritten card expressing first her grief for Linda losing her husband and then gratitude to her for gifting her husband's heart so her husband had a chance to live. In this note, Candace included her phone number, asking Linda to give her a call when she felt ready. Candace sent the flowers yesterday, and she was hoping that Linda would contact her at some point soon. Betsy had just arrived at the house, as she and her mother were getting ready to go see Chip at the hospital.

The phone rang. Candace picked up the phone and said *hello*; on the other end was Linda.

"Hello, is this Candace?"

Candace replied, "Yes, this is she." Candace recognized Linda's voice immediately.

"I just wanted to thank you for the lovely flowers Candace, but it wasn't necessary," said Linda.

"Linda, how are you getting along? Do you need anything?" replied Candace.

"Well, all things considered, I'm doing okay. How is your husband doing?"

Candace said, "He's doing very well, thank you. Betsy and I are going to go see him in a few minutes."

Linda replied, "I'm so happy that he's doing well. Make sure you tell him I said *hello*."

Candace then said, "Linda, I know Chip is going to want to meet and thank you personally. After he gets home, could I or Betsy pick you up and have you come over to see him and have dinner with us?"

With a slight pause, Linda replied, "I would like that very much. It would be nice to spend time with someone. I've been pretty lonely, and I really don't know the people Bo worked with, so other than a few notes from them…yes I'd love to come over, as long as I won't be imposing?"

Candace first thought to herself, *Imposing?* She then replied, "It will be very nice seeing you. We'll find out today when Chip's coming home, so I'll give you a call, and we'll set things up. In the meantime, anytime, anytime at all, if you need something or just wish to talk, please don't hesitate. I want to be available to you."

Linda happily responded, "Thank you, Candace, I just may do that, and I'll look forward to hearing from you, but now, go see your husband, and again remember to give him my best."

"I will, and thank you," replied Candace. With that, both women hung up the phone, and Candace, while heading to the door with Betsy, said, "Linda is a remarkable woman. We really must help her any way we can."

With that, the women left the house.

# Chapter 26

Arriving in Chip's room, there were two nurses with Chip. Candace was startled but quickly realized it was just a nurse checking his vitals (this was just routine), and the other was an orderly removing Chip's breakfast tray. As they walked in, the nurse and orderly left the room.

Chip smiled and said to Candace, "Hey, sweetie, let me look at you!" Turning to his daughter, he said, "Hello, honey, you both look great!"

The three of them started making small talk, the ladies asking Chip how he was feeling and Chip responding in kind. Then Chip's doctor came into the room. Knocking on the door before entering, the doctor said, "Hello, am I late for the party?"

All three laughed as the doctor walked to the foot of the bed. "I have some good news for all of you. Chip, you can go home tomorrow."

The three of them all smiled as Candace took Chip's hand. The doctor said, "All is looking good, and you're ahead of schedule recoverywise. I don't want you to think, Chip, that you can hit the course with your clubs, not yet."

Chip responded, "10–4, Doc."

As the doctor left the room, the three proceeded to discuss plans for Chip's homecoming. Betsy said, "Daddy, is there anything you'd like to eat? It's been a few weeks since you had any real food."

Chip turned to Candace and said, "Sweetie, could you find out from my nurse if they have a list of food that I can eat? I don't want to torture myself wanting something they won't let me have. After you find that out, I'll make my list of food demands," Chip said with a laugh.

Candace responded, "Okay, we'll ask on our way out."

After a short visit, the women stood up to leave. "Get some rest, and we'll see you tomorrow morning," said Candace.

Betsy leaned over to kiss her father goodbye, saying, "Until tomorrow morning, Daddy."

"Can't wait honey," said Chip.

Candace then leaned over to kiss Chip; before she could, Chip said, "I love you sweetie, see you in the morning, and Candy, things are going to be different."

With that, Candace opened Chip's hand and placed the silver coin in his hand.

"What's this?" said Chip.

Candace told him, "It was by your pillow the other day, just before you went in for the transplant. I figured someone put it there for good luck."

"Hey, what do you think about that?" said Chip, "a good luck charm."

She then smiled at Chip, kissed him on the lips, and said, "I love you, Chip, see you tomorrow." The girls then turned to leave. Again Candace's mind was racing, replaying to herself what Chip said, "Things will be different." Candace could only hope.

# Chapter 27

The next morning, there was excitement in the Thayer home; Chip was coming home. Candace hurried around getting ready, and Betsy was waiting for her downstairs.

"C'mon Mom, what are you doing up there?" As Betsy said this, Candace came walking down the stairs, putting on her earing.

"Okay okay, here I am," said Candace.

Betsy said, "Mom, I know this sounds nuts, but I'm nervous with excitement," letting out a little giggle.

Candace smiled at her and said, "So am I honey, so am I." The two ladies then left the house, got into the car, and left for the hospital.

# Chapter 28

Arriving at the hospital, the two women were in the waiting area as Chip went through the release checkup by his physician, and if all was good, they'd be permitted to take him home. The women were anxious with hope. Chip had come through this ordeal very well, but he still had quite a way to go before he'd be back at full strength. The thing that kept passing through Candace's mind though was Chip calling her *sweetie*. He had never said that to her in all the years they've known each other, and the coincidence was too great. Then from down the hall came Chip. He was in a wheelchair, being pushed by an orderly.

As they approached the two women, the orderly asked, "Is your car out front? I'll wheel him to it."

Both women nodded affirmatively and said at the same time, "Yes."

The four then left the hospital to where Candace's car was parked. The orderly went to assist Chip into the front passenger seat, when Chip said, "Let the ladies sit up front. I'll ride in the back."

The orderly helped him into the back seat, the three of them thanked the orderly, and Candace pulled away. Chip said in a louder voice than the girls thought he had strength for, "Hot dang! Am I happy to be getting out of there!"

The two ladies laughed at Chip's exuberance. As Candace was driving, she then said, "Chip, we are planning a nice dinner, well, as nice as the diet the doctor laid out for you will allow. Don't worry, you'll be back eating anything you want soon."

Chip replied, "Sweetie, anything will be better than what I had in there, plus maybe it's time I changed a few of my eating and drinking habits."

*Again, with the* sweetie, Candace thought as she looked at Chip in the rearview mirror.

Betsy chimed in, "Dad, we're going to eat the same meals as you, at least while I'm here at home. At school, I'll just have to live on whatever gruel they have. We all need to start taking better care of ourselves."

Chip replied, "Honeybunch, you're young. Enjoy yourself. Eat and drink whatever you want. Just do it in moderation."

The car became quiet as now the two women were in their own thoughts with Betsy thinking to herself, *He really has changed.*

They were almost home now, and Chip was talking away happily, seemingly making up for lost time, when Candace said, "Chip, I've got to tell you something."

"What's that, sweetie?" replied Chip.

"I met a woman at the hospital that was in the waiting area with me. You could tell by the way she dressed and the way she spoke of herself and her husband that they really didn't have much, you know, materialwise, that is."

She paused a bit, and Chip said, "Yeah, go on."

Now Candace, with her voice suddenly rising, said, "Chip, this woman may be the most generous and unassuming person I've ever met."

"Why's that," said Chip.

"She was continually asking how you were doing. In the meantime, her husband wasn't getting any better, and well, he passed away."

Chip replied, "Oh, I'm sorry to hear that." Then Chip continued, "Why are you telling me this, sweetie?"

Candace was trying to compose herself, when she started to lightly cry and said, "A doctor came out and took her into his office. While in the office, we could see that she began to cry. The doctor was talking, and then we saw her nod her head up and down, and she signed a paper. They then took her back to see her husband. When she came out, she was crying. A nurse walking with her said something to her, and she shook her head *no*. With that, she came over to us, and when we asked her what had happened, she told us that they couldn't save her husband and they took her back to say *goodbye*. I hugged her, and Betsy offered to drive her home, when she said, 'No, you need to be here with your mother. She and your father need your support.' She then left."

Chip appeared confused, "Candy, that's sad, but why are you telling me this?"

Then Candace swallowed hard and said, "Chip, your new heart was her husband's. She signed a paper right then to donate it, and she knew it was going into you, but at the time, we didn't. We didn't find out until later."

Chip sat there and said, "My god, we've got to get ahold of her, I've got to show my gratitude to her in person." The car remained quiet for the remainder of the drive home, all three of them lost in their thoughts.

# Chapter 29

Back at the house, Chip and Betsy were sitting at the dining room table while Candace prepared some lunch. Chip was twirling his new good luck charm in his left hand as he asked Betsy how things were going at school.

Betsy then asked her father, "Daddy, what's that you're holding?"

Chip responded, "Your mother found this on my bed in the hospital. I guess it's my new good luck charm. Still, if I knew who it belonged to, I'd want to give it back to them. It's an older coin, and it's all silver. Someone is probably wondering where they lost it."

Candace then walked in from the kitchen, carrying lunch. "Anyone hungry?" she asked. Both Chip and Betsy raised their hands.

While they sat and ate, the subject of Linda came up. Chip began, "Candy, do you know how to contact Linda?"

Candace replied, "Yes, I spoke with her once on the telephone, and I mentioned to her that she should contact me if she needed anything. I also said that we'd like to have her over once you were home and strong enough for visitors."

Chip replied, "Then please call her. I'm strong enough right now to meet that woman."

With that, they continued eating their lunch.

# Chapter 30

After lunch, Betsy left to go to class, and Chip went to take a nap. Candace was cleaning up from lunch, then planned on calling Linda to invite her over. Once she finished in the kitchen, Candace sat down by the phone and paused for a minute, thinking of what she wanted to say to Linda. Candace was surprised upon realizing that she actually missed Linda's company. She brought calm to Candace at a very rough time. Candace also thought that Linda must be a very strong-willed person, perhaps stronger than she had thought of herself. Candace picked up the phone and began to dial. While doing this, she looked at the clock; it was twenty past two. The phone began to ring, and Candace actually became quite nervous. After ten or twelve rings, Candace hung up. She then remembered that Linda worked at a store, and perhaps that's where she was. "I'll call her back tonight," she said to herself and hung up the phone.

# Chapter 31

That evening after dinner, Chip was watching the news on TV. It was a quarter past seven, when Candace decided to give Linda another try. This time Linda was home and picked up the phone.

"Hello?" Candace quickly responded. "Hello, Linda, this is Candace."

Linda replied, "Oh hello, it's nice of you to call. How's your husband doing?"

Candace replied, "He's doing very well, thank you for asking. As a matter of fact, he'd very much like to meet you. That's why I'm calling. Would you like to come over for dinner tomorrow?"

Linda didn't even pause, "That would be very nice, but I don't know if the bus runs near your neighborhood."

Candace replied, "I have your address, and either Betsy or I will pick you up and then take you home afterward. Does that sound good with you?"

Linda replied, "That'd be very nice of you. I'd like that very much. Is there anything you'd like me to bring?"

Candace quickly thought, *This woman thinks of everyone but herself.* "Not at all, we'll have a nice dinner and visit afterward." Candace then asked Linda, "What would you like for dinner?"

"Oh my, anything would be lovely. Please don't go out of your way. I get home from work around six. Is that okay? I hope that doesn't inconvenience you?"

"It's no problem. How would six thirty work for you? We will pick you up then."

Linda replied, "That sounds fine. I'll be waiting outside, because I live on the upstairs of the business below, and I don't want you to have to get out of your car to come up and ring the bell."

Again, Candace thought, *This woman's always thinking of others.* Candace was now happy and excited. "Perfect, either Betsy or I will be there to pick you up at six thirty. Until tomorrow, have a nice evening, and Linda, we're really looking forward to having you come over."

Linda replied, "Candace, I'm looking forward to tomorrow night also."

With that, both women hung up.

# Chapter 32

The next evening, Candace was buzzing around between the kitchen and dining room, getting everything ready. Chip was in the living room talking on the phone, and Betsy had arrived home from school in time to give her mother a hand getting everything ready. It almost seemed like Christmas with the anticipation that was in the Thayer home that evening.

Chip came walking into the kitchen and said to Candace, "I just got off the phone with Zach Hall (*his business partner*), and, sweetie, if it isn't too much trouble for you, I'd like to go into the office tomorrow. It won't take any more than an hour. Would you take me in and wait for me? I called a board meeting with the directors. I promise, no more than one hour."

Candace turned to him and asked, "Are you sure you're up to it?"

Chip nodded and said, "I think I'll be all right. I've got to address the group; it's time this company became involved in things other than just worrying about the bottom line."

Candace was surprised, but maybe not surprised by her husband's comments and the new way he was approaching things. Candace answered, "Sure Chip, listen to me and please listen to what I'm saying. When Linda comes over, please don't call me *sweetie* in front of her."

Chip looked at Candace, somewhat perplexed, and said, "Why's that?"

Candace took Chip by both arms and looked him directly in the eye and said, "That's what Linda's husband, Bo, called her. I think it may open up a wound if she hears you calling me that."

Then Candace smiled and said, "Of course, I love hearing it any other time."

Chip, with a serious look on his face, shook his head up and down in agreement.

Chip then turned to go back into the living room when Betsy came into the kitchen and said, "Mom, it's time to pick Linda up. Why don't you go, and I'll stay and watch the roast and finish things up here. You and Linda could have a nice talk on the way back."

Candace replied, "Thanks, honey, that's a good idea. While I'm thinking about it, do you have a class tomorrow? Your sister's flying in, and your father wants me to take him to his office in the morning."

Betsy replied, "Sure thing."

With that, Candace grabbed her coat and headed out to her car.

# Chapter 33

As Candace left the house, she got in her Mercedes-Benz S580, and as she drove to pick up Linda, she was filled with excitement and sorrow. For Candace, it appeared life was finally going to be as she always hoped. Chip had turned into the person she always thought he could be, with all the good things that would come with it, but at the same time, she felt so sad for Linda. Alone, with no friends, and no longer having the company of her husband, she became determined to include Linda in their circles from this point forward. Driving along, as she was getting closer to the neighborhood where Linda lived, it seemed to grow darker and darker, as if the street lighting was as poor as the neighborhood Linda lived in.

As she arrived in the area where Linda resided, the street lighting seemed dim, and Candace squinted, looking for the building with the barbershop on the first floor. As Candace got close, she saw a figure standing in front of the building; it was Linda. Candace pulled right up to her and lowered the passenger side window and said, "Hi, Linda."

Linda got into the car, and the two women leaned toward each other to give a hug. Candace surprised herself at how open she was with her new friend, as she hadn't been close with anyone she'd known her entire life, save her daughters. As they broke their embrace, Candace started to drive back toward her home, asking Linda how she'd been getting along.

Linda replied, "Candace, it's been very rough. It's been okay during the day, while at work. As a matter of fact, the people there have been much friendlier to me since, well, you know. But at night, when I'm home alone, is when things get tough. I've been trying to keep busy, either reading or watching TV, and I've recently taken up knitting. Still the quiet is bothersome. I'd rather be talking with someone more than anything."

Candace then said, "Tonight we'll have dinner and some nice conversation, and Chip's really been looking forward to meeting you."

With that, Linda smiled and sat comfortably as Candace continued the drive to her home.

## Chapter 34

As they pulled into the driveway of the Thayer home, Linda's jaw just dropped. She'd never seen a house quite like this, with a brick front and several roof peaks, the whole yard glowing with landscape lighting, a circular driveway, and on the side a four-car garage. Candace pulled halfway up on the circular drive, stopping right near the front door of the home. The women exited the car, walked up to the front door, and entered the home. Linda looked around and was in total awe by what she saw.

Linda said to Candace, "My, you have a lovely home."

Candace smiled, "Thank you, let me take your coat."

The women walked in, and Candace asked Linda to have a seat. Betsy came into the living room and smiled at Linda, "Hello, Mrs. Shott, how've you been?"

Linda stood and replied, "Oh, pretty well, I guess. You look lovely, Betsy."

"You're too kind, please sit down," Betsy replied.

"Is your sister, Amy, here?" Linda asked.

"She's coming into town tomorrow. I'll be picking her up at the airport in the morning."

Candace then left the room to collect Chip. They returned to the living room, and Linda stood again. Candace gratefully made the introduction. "Linda, this is my husband, Chip."

Chip walked right up to Linda, reaching out to her and saying, "I'm so pleased to finally meet you," giving Linda a hug. Linda was almost shy in her response, and both Candace and Betsy were surprised by the affection Chip showed. Affection wasn't one of his strong points, but they both knew this was a new Chip.

As Chip and Linda completed their introduction, Betsy said, "I hope everyone's hungry. I think dinner's ready."

The four of them sat down at the dinner table. Already on their dinner plates was a small glass bowl with five large shrimp. Candace then asked Linda, "I'm sorry that I didn't think of asking you beforehand. I hope you aren't allergic to shellfish?"

Linda chuckled, "Well, I don't know. I've never had shrimp before."

The other three shared a quick look of surprise, with Betsy saying, "Ma'am, the red sauce is cocktail sauce. It's supposed to be a bit spicy, so you may want to give it a little taste first."

With that, Linda dipped her pinky into the sauce and tasted it. "Woo, spicy, but I like it!"

The other three laughed. Then Linda asked Betsy for a favor. "Betsy, would you please call me *Linda*? Ma'am and Mrs. Shott make me feel kind of uncomfortable," she said with a chuckle. "Everyone I work with just calls me Linda."

Betsy replied, "Certainly, if that's what you'd like."

After they disposed of their shrimp appetizers, which Linda thought was incredible, Candace brought in the main course: standing rib roast, roasted potatoes, and asparagus with hollandaise sauce. Linda never saw a piece of meat that large, and the aroma was incredible. "I hope you're hungry, Linda, because Chip is having very small portions," she said with a laugh.

Chip laughed himself and replied, "Please, Mommy, I've been a good boy." They all got a laugh out of that.

As they ate, Linda thought to herself, *This was the most delicious meal she'd ever eaten*, but refrained to comment until dinner was done. She felt commenting too soon may be rude. With dinner now finished, they stood, going into the living room. Linda stood with her clean plate and said, "Let me help with the dishes."

Betsy replied, "Nonsense, we'll get these later. Would anyone like coffee?"

They all had a very enjoyable evening, when Linda looked at her watch—the last gift she received from Bo, a Timex. "I've had a wonderful time, but I better call a taxi. I have to work tomorrow. Candace, I can help you with the dishes until my ride arrives."

Betsy chimed in, "Mrs., I'm sorry, Linda, I'll drive you home. I have to go back to my dorm, and from what Mom told me, it's in the same direction."

Linda responded, "That would be very nice of you, Betsy, but let's first help your mother with the dishes."

Chip stood and said, "Nonsense, Candace and I will get them."

Candace turned to Chip and smiled. With that, they all stood, as Chip retrieved Linda's coat, helping her with it. Linda, now embarrassed, smiled and said, "I really want to thank you for a wonderful evening. This has been the best night I have had in quite some time."

Chip replied, "Linda, I have a feeling this is just the first of many times we'll spend together. You're always welcome here."

With that, goodbye hugs went all around, and Linda and Betsy headed for the door. As they left, hearing the car leave the driveway, Candace turned to Chip and said, "What did I tell you, she's a remarkable woman."

As they began to take the dishes from the table to the kitchen, Chip said, "I've got to do something for her, and at tomorrow's board meeting, I think I know what I'm going to do."

Candace said, "As long as you can get it done in one hour. You know what the doctor said."

"Candy, stay there for one hour and drag me out if necessary. I won't fight you." She smiled and shook her head up and down. Chip smiled back, "That's my sweetie," as they took the remaining plates to the kitchen.

# Chapter 35

The next morning, there was a buzz around the office of Thayer Commercial Development. The main man was coming in after his long absence to check on and probably scrutinize what's been happening since his absence, or so the people at the office thought. Two members of the development team were talking. Trevor Alexander, the new whiz kid of the company, idolized Chip Thayer. He wasn't too enthusiastic about Chip's methods, but you couldn't argue with his success. When Trevor was done speaking, Matt DePasquale chimed in. Matt had been with the company longer than Trevor and hadn't near the success as he had. He also wasn't too fond of Chip and didn't mind speaking his mind. Chip never gave Matt the time of day and only tolerated him as Matt was the stepson of his partner, Zach Hall. "Well, the old man returns today. Great, I'll bet he's going to look around and tear everyone a new asshole." As he spoke, other employees filed in, with Zach Hall walking in quickly.

Turning to Trevor and Matt, he said, "Have everyone go into the large conference room. Chip wants to speak with all of us."

Trevor responded, "Yes, Mr. Hall."

Matt just shook his head. "Great, vacation's over."

A short time later, Chip and Candace entered the office. Chip's secretary, Valerie, came over to him, handing Chip a bouquet of flowers with a *Welcome Back*! card attached. To Valerie's surprise, Chip gave her a thank you hug. He then turned and looked around the office and said, "Ah, the place looks great."

Valerie responded, "Everyone's here, and they are eagerly awaiting your arrival in the large conference room."

"Well," said Chip, "I don't want to keep everyone waiting." He then turned to Valerie and said, "Synchronize your watch. If I'm still yapping after one hour, come in and drag me out." With that, Chip entered the conference room.

As Chip entered, Zach Hall stood to give him a standing ovation; others followed, some patronizingly so. Chip noticed this, but thought quickly to himself, *I deserve that*. As they lined up to welcome him individually, he felt grateful for their warm response but more so now wanted and was in the position to do great things. He motioned for everyone to sit down, then proceeded to describe what he'd been through surgically and during his convalescence. He then turned his attention to his reason for calling them all together this morning. Chip began by saying how wrong he'd been on his views of both volunteering and donating to worthy causes.

"I've changed," Chip declared. "It's taken a life-threatening event for me to make that change, but often good things are born from bad." He continued, "We have a very successful business here, ladies and gentlemen, and it's time we give back. The growth of our company must always be foremost in our efforts, as the more success we have will allow us to become more involved in the assistance of those in society that really need help. I've come to realize there are very good people in our society that either have had a bad go at it, a run of bad luck, or just never had the opportunity to achieve success. Therefore, I will be meeting with Mr. Hall this week, and we'll be forming a charitable foundation, of course, pending the approval of the board of directors, with the name and goals we hope to achieve. With doctor's orders and my wife waiting out in the lobby, I'll be going home now. Everyone, continue to do the excellent job that you've been doing, and I'll be looking forward to the company's award banquet a week from this Saturday. At the banquet, we'll roll out the name, description, and goals of the new foundation. It's been great being here today, and I look forward to being back here on a full-time basis." Chip then waived to everyone and turned to leave.

The others stood and gave Chip a nice round of applause. Matt, who was seated next to Trevor, said to him as they stood to leave, "I don't know what they put in him, but he's sure changed."

# Chapter 36

Arriving back home, Betsy and Amy were waiting for them. Amy cautiously approached her father, as the last time she was in his presence and conscious, Chip was somewhat cool—as he'd always been toward her. "Hi, Daddy, how are you feeling?"

As Chip walked toward Amy, he opened his arms and said, "Hello, honey, I'm so happy you're here."

Amy noticed tears in Chip's eyes as they embraced. All the years of animosity that Amy had for her father melted away in their embrace. Chip then leaned back, looking her over. "My god, you look beautiful."

Amy didn't recognize this in her father, but she ate it up. Laughing, she said, "Daddy, you look tremendous. How are you feeling?"

"Stronger every day, baby, stronger every day." With that, Chip and his two daughters sat down to get caught up. Candace went into the kitchen to prepare some lunch. While they ate, they all talked and laughed and reminisced. All three of the women were surprised by the things he recalled. They never thought he'd recall anything from the past as he never seemed to pay attention to them back then, except for some of the things with Betsy.

After about an hour, Chip said, "Well, all this excitement has gotten me a bit tired. I think I'll grab me a little nap." Chip got up and left for the bedroom.

The women cleaned up the lunch dishes and sat back down and quietly talked. Betsy went first, "I'm so happy Daddy's doing well. The day we brought him home from the hospital, he looked like he'd aged twenty years. Now he looks ten years younger than when he went in."

Amy chimed in, "The change in him is remarkable. He's like a new man."

Candace then said, "My emotions are so screwed up. I'm so angry at myself. When we were at the hospital and before we heard that your father was going to need a new heart, I almost felt bothered having to be there. Then I met Linda and saw the love she had for her husband and then her losing him. It was so unfair, especially finding out that she signed papers allowing them to put her husband's heart in the chest of your father. I prayed to God, not only for your father's recovery, but also that with the new heart, he'd become a changed man. I'm so selfish."

Amy quickly replied, "No, you aren't, Mother. He treated you like a second-class citizen for years. This change in him is remarkable, and not only does the change give him a second chance in life, but also it finally gives you the chance for some well-deserved happiness. The thing that really sucks is how Linda's loss has become our gain. It just isn't fair."

Betsy nodded in agreement and said, "Mom, Linda is like a savior, and I hope you and Dad never forget that."

Candace then said, "Your father has something in mind for Linda, something big. He told me earlier that he wants to speak to me about it sometime tomorrow after he gets the chance to formulate his idea and get it down on paper."

With that, the girls leaned back, with Candace asking the girls questions about what's been new in their lives.

# Chapter 37

The next morning, Chip and Candace were just finishing breakfast, and as he stood up from the table he said to Candace, "I'll be in the office finishing up what my plans are for the foundation. Once I finish, I'd like to go over it with you. If you like the idea, I'd like us to have Linda here for dinner and present it to her. Before that, I want to run it by Zach Hall. I think he'll like the idea. After all, he was the most vocal in the past on my reluctance for us getting involved with charitable functions."

Candace replied, "Okay, but if you run long, I want you to take a break for lunch and then a nap. We can go over it later, and you can call Zach later tonight and tell him that you'd like for him to stop over at some point tomorrow."

Chip smiled at her, "Sure thing, sweetie."

Chip turned and headed to his office, as Candace smiled and watched him walk away.

Later, as Chip came out of his office with a bounce in his step, he called out to Candace, "Candy, I think I've got it finished. Come here, and let's go over it."

Out she came from the kitchen, drying her hands in a kitchen towel as she walked. "Can't this wait until after dinner?" she said.

Chip then began, "Candy, this won't take long, so let's hold off dinner for a while, if that's okay with you?"

Candace replied, "Yeah, sure."

With great detail and excitement, Chip went on to describe what the foundation's goals will be and how he wanted Linda as the head of the organization, with the help of a full-time assistant. He had a person in mind for this, Jayne Arko, a woman who worked with Chip a few years back, a very intelligent and driven woman who was rising fast in his commercial development company but had to leave after she had given birth to her third child, a child born with both physical and mental disabilities.

"Yes," said Candace, "I think Jayne would be a perfect fit. Intelligent, organized, motivated—she's the perfect person for this. Do you think she'd be interested?"

Chip responded, "I already contacted her, and she didn't even hesitate. Jayne said, 'What a wonderful thing you and Candace are doing.'"

Candace then said, "It all sounds great Chip, but do you think Linda will have the time to do this, with her job and all, or were you planning on paying her?"

Chip turned and chuckled, "Oh, I think it's time for her to put in her notice at the store, and yes, I'm going to pay her. How does a six figure salary sound?"

Candace was shocked. "Wow, Chip, that's very generous of you. Do you think Zach Hall and the other board members will go for it?"

"Hey, I'm still the boss. If the others have a problem with it, I'll make assurances that we'll make it work. Even if I have to pay her out of my own pocket." Turning to Candace he said, "I've got another chance at life to do good, good for others and not just my own selfish self."

Candace was quiet, he then smiled broadly and said, "Sweetie, we can still have a long happy life, and if we can help others in the process, what could be better?"

Candace smiled back; then a serious look came to her face. "Chip, Linda is such a loyal person. Do you think she'd leave her job at the store?"

Chip paused and thought for a moment and said, "I never gave that much thought. I hope so. I guess I may have to do my first selling job since my illness. Hand me the phone. I want to give Zach a call."

# Chapter 38

The next afternoon, as Chip waited for Zach Hall to arrive, he was finishing up his proposal. If he could sell the idea to Zach, he was sure the other board members would go for it. Chip and Zach were generally on the same page businesswise; it was Chip's prior reluctance of getting involved with donations to charities and various social causes that they couldn't agree on. Basically, Chip was a very cold and selfish person, which Zach normally dealt with because of their business success, of which Chip was a master.

Chip was now seated in the living room, and Candace brought out some coffee and light sandwiches so Chip and Zach could have a bite while going over Chip's proposal. As Candace set down the sandwich tray, the doorbell rang. Chip stood up and said, "I'll get it."

He then opened the door, and in walked Zach, giving Chip a smile and a handshake. "Man, you're looking great, how you feeling?"

Chip said, "Stronger every day. As a matter of fact, I'm planning on returning to the office on Monday, for half a day, until I feel strong enough to do more hours."

The two sat down, and Candace said, "I'll leave you two alone. Just give me a yell if you need anything."

Chip reached out to take her arm and said, "Candy, I want you to be a part of this."

The three of them sat down, and as Chip went over his proposal, Zach was in total agreement and felt that he could take it to the board for approval. "It all sounds great Chip, and I think the board will agree to this. As you know, they have been wanting to become involved in something like this for quite some time. As for the assistant, I think Jayne Arko is a perfect fit. The only question is, 'Will she be willing to return to work?'" asked Zach.

"Well, I also plan on compensating Jayne appropriately if she agrees, and she'll be an integral part of the foundation. With her drive and intellect, I know she'll be the perfect right arm for Linda, and I believe the two of them will get along quite well. While I'm here working from home, if the board gives its approval, I'll begin making phone calls, trying to get some of our affiliates to pledge donations. My plan is to present the concept of the foundation with the goals we intend to achieve and introduce our president and CEO at our annual banquet a week from this Saturday. If you can roust up the board for a conference and the sooner the better, we'll get this off the ground."

Zach then stood and said, "I'll call the board members as soon as I get home. Candace, I want to thank you for the sandwiches and coffee. They were delicious."

Chip and Zach then walked to the front door, and while shaking hands, Chip said, "Please sell this to the board. I really want to move this on."

Zach smiled and said, "I honestly think it will be just a formality, and I'll call you as soon as we can meet and get their approval. Good night, Chip, I'll be in touch."

With that, Chip closed the door, walked over to Candace, and gave her a hug. "Sweetie, I want you to give Linda a call and invite her for dinner tomorrow night. See if Amy can pick her up, and ask Betsy if she's available. I'd like everyone here."

Candace said, "Chip, shouldn't you wait for the board's approval on this? We can have Linda over in a day or two."

Chip shook his head and said, "The board has wanted to do something like this for quite some time. It was me who always derailed it. I really want to get Linda to agree on this and get the ball rolling." Then looking right into Candace's eyes, he said, "I've wasted enough time, and it's time to make up for it."

Candace and Chip then embraced.

# Chapter 39

It was two thirty the next afternoon when Chip received a call from Zach that the board was unanimous in moving forward with Chip's foundation proposal. He was very excited when talking with Zach.

"Excellent," said Chip. "Now, Zach, you contact the attorneys and get the whole thing set up. You have all the necessary paperwork that I'd been working on. As for the president and CEO, I hope that I'll have that resolved this evening. Let's move this on. I want to have everything in order by the banquet."

Zach, almost laughing at Chip's exuberance, said, "Okay, okay, now if you can shut up and let me get started."

Chip hesitated ever so slightly and said, "You're right, get going, and I'll call you right after we meet with Linda. She's coming over for dinner tonight. Talk with you later."

Chip hung up without even a goodbye, and Zach just shook his head and laughed as he hung up the phone.

It was quarter to seven when Linda and Amy came into the home. Betsy was on the sofa, talking with her father, and Candace was in the kitchen. With the sound of the door opening, Betsy and Chip stood up, and Candace came from the kitchen. *Hellos* and *hugs* went to Linda from the three, and then they sat down for a small talk, with Candace saying, "Dinner will be ready in just a few minutes."

Turning to Chip, she motioned, as if to ask if he was going to say anything now. Chip shook his head and mimed, "After dinner."

At dinner, there was a lot of chatter. Linda was becoming more at ease, and Amy, always being the standoffish one, was becoming more in touch with her softer side, this being the result of the goodness she had witnessed, not only from Linda but also from her father. *Miracles all around*, she thought. This woman's generosity, giving the heart of her deceased husband, the acceptance of her father's body not rejecting the heart placed inside him, and the incredible change in her father's level of kindness made this gathering such an enjoyable experience. With dinner now over, they adjourned to the living room for coffee and for more conversation. Linda was seated on the large sofa between Chip and Candace, and the two girls sat down in the large easy chairs.

After a few minutes of more light conversation, Chip now began, "Linda, the company that I inherited from my father has been successful for a very long time. For years our board of directors has been after me to have our company become involved in some type of charitable foundation, with all their ideas dying at my desk. Since this sojourn that I've just been through, it's finally entered my mind that this isn't only something we should be a part of, but an idea we should embrace."

Chip now looked at his family and then continued. "Linda, with the agreement of our board of directors, we are starting a foundation. We are calling it the *Robert and Linda Schott Foundation for the Less Fortunate*, and we want you to be an integral part of this."

Linda responded, "That sounds very nice, and I'm honored, as I'm sure Bo would be. It's very generous of you and your company, but what could I do?"

"Linda, I need to ask you this first. Would you be willing to leave your job to head this foundation?"

"I don't know," said Linda. "I need the income to live, and as much as I'd love to help in any way possible, I still need to work."

With that, the four Thayers looked at each other and smiled. "Linda, I'd like you to be president and chief executive officer of the foundation. We are going to pay you a salary of $100,000 a year. Would this change your mind about leaving your job?"

Linda sat there in shock, not speaking for a good fifteen seconds, then said, "I wouldn't know what to do. How could you pay me that kind of money? What if I don't do a good job, where would I begin?"

Chip then said, "Yesterday, I spoke with the individual who'll be signing on as your assistant, pending your acceptance to the position.

Her name is Jayne Arko, and she's been an outstanding member of our company but has been away from the company for several years as she needed to take a personal sabbatical from her career. When I contacted Jayne regarding our idea for the foundation and what it was going to be for, describing what our goals would be and telling her the wonderful woman she'd be assisting, she said, 'I'm all in.' Jayne will be working with and teaching you everything you need to learn. I'll be honest, it will be time-consuming, and you'll need to work at this to help make it successful."

Linda then said, "I'd love to do something to help, and it sure seems like it will keep me busy. I've been spending too many quiet, lonely hours." Smiling, she added, "But the money is far too generous."

"Nonsense," said Chip. "Your generosity is far greater, and you deserve this more than you'll ever know." Then Chip leaned over, taking Linda by the hand. "Don't you think Bo would want this for you?"

Linda, now becoming somewhat emotional, said, "I know he always did the best he could for me, and I wish he was here to be a part of this."

Chip then looked Linda in the eye, took her hand and placed it on his heart, and said, "He is here, and he very much wants this for you."

With this, all the women in the room became emotional, and Linda, after wiping away a tear, said, "Thank you, I thank you, and so does Bo. I accept."

Chip then stood up and, still holding Linda by the hand, helped her stand, and he gave her a hug. Then Candace, Amy, and Betsy came over with hugs going all around. Linda then asked, "Can I perform my first act as president?"

Chip said, "Sure thing, what would you like?"

Linda then said, "I'd like 20% of my salary to be donated to the foundation."

Chip laughed and said, "Yes, Madame President, if you so wish."

The four of them laughed, with Candace just looking and saying to herself, "This woman is remarkable."

# Chapter 40

Late the following afternoon, as Candace and Chip were just puttering around the house, there was a ring of the doorbell. They looked at each other and shrugged. Neither of them expected anyone, and as Candace went to answer the door, Chip sat down with the newspaper. As Candace opened the door, to Candace's surprise, there stood Brian. As he stepped in, he gave his sister a hug.

"How's he doing?" said Brian, not mentioning Chip by name.

*The coolness was still there*, Candace noticed. "Chip's doing well," she said, making certain to say his name.

Chip, now hearing them talk, stood up and walked to the door. When he saw Brian, he said rather loudly, "Hey Brian, get in here!" Chip met him halfway and grasped Brian by both shoulders and said, "Kid, you look great."

Being taken aback at Chip's welcome, Brian responded, "You're looking a hellova' lot better than the last time I saw you."

Chip just laughed and said, "I imagine so. C'mon in and have a seat."

The three of them had a nice visit, just over an hour, as Brian stood up to leave. "I best get going." He then shook Chip's hand and said, "Get better, old man, the links are calling your name."

Chip laughed and said, "As soon as the doctor gives me the green light, I'll give you a call and we'll get out there."

As Candace walked Brian to the door, he turned to her and said, "I'm not sure who the hell this guy is, but I sure like him."

Candace just laughed and kissed her brother on the cheek. "Thanks for coming, Brian. Please stop by anytime. I'm sure Chip would love to see you again soon."

Brian smiled and said, "All right, I'll see you both again soon."

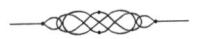

# Chapter 41

Several days passed, and Linda spent her day hours in the newly remodeled section of the office where the foundation was to be operating from. Linda was being instructed by Jayne on the various issues they needed to grasp hold of to get the new foundation off the ground. The two women hit it off immediately, burying themselves over what was needed once they really got the ball rolling. Getting to know one another, it seemed they had similar upbringings, with Jayne coming from a rather poor family but not having the social obstacles that Linda had gone through. Linda was having trouble grasping much of the terminology, but with Jayne's tutelage and patience, things were coming along at a steady pace.

Jayne told her, "Linda, this is why I'm here. Of course, you're not going to understand this right off. Much of this is new to me, but as time goes by, you'll pick this up and be as proficient at this as me. Let's just work hard and have fun."

Linda has enjoyed the challenge and the way it has filled her time. The evenings, thus far, had been filled with her going over the ins and outs of what running a foundation entails, and with the added income, she has not had to worry about affording the day-to-day things that were always a part of her daily troubles. Just before breaking for lunch, much to their surprise, Chip and Candace stuck their heads in to say *hello*.

"How's it going in here?" Chip cheerfully asked.

After some small talk, Candace pulled Linda aside and said, "Linda, after lunch, I'd like to take you shopping for something new to wear for the banquet."

Linda quickly agreed. She knew she had nothing to wear that would make her look anything more than a cleaning person picking up afterward, and she'd been so busy working both at the office and in the evening at home that she hadn't had the opportunity to shop for clothes. Besides, she had no idea where to shop as all her clothes were not purchased anywhere except secondhand shops, other than the lovely sweater that Bo bought for her, that she wore almost constantly.

"That would be very nice of you," said Linda.

At the women's clothing store, Candace thought they should find Linda something very professional, but feminine. Linda was leaving all this upon Candace, as she had really no idea what to look for. After several outfits were brought to Linda, she tried them on, coming out of the dressing room, looking for Candace's approval. After each outfit, Candace would say, "Maybe, try the next one on."

Linda would look at herself in the dressing room mirror and say, "I have no clue as to what I'm supposed to look like, but I hope Candace agrees on something very humble."

Finally, they found a nice simple business suit Linda was happy with and had hoped Candace also approved of. Linda walked out of the dressing room, looking for Candace's thoughts.

"Yes, this outfit looks terrific, and it looks great on you."

Turning to the saleswoman, Candace said. "We'll take this one."

As they headed to the checkout area, Linda reached into her purse for cash. She now had some money but had no credit cards to her name, something that she'd hoped to soon rectify. Candace then placed her hands on Linda's purse. "No, this one's on me. Some Saturday I'll take you shopping for a whole new wardrobe—you're going to need one. We'll have lunch and make a whole day of it."

"That'll be fun Candace, and thank you for this."

Candace then smiled and gave Linda a hug and said, "No, Linda, thank you."

# Chapter 42

The day of the company banquet arrived. Linda was milling about her little three-room apartment, nervously thinking about the change in her life that was going to occur tonight. The event was to begin at seven, but Chip was having a car pick her up at five thirty, as he wanted to introduce her to the board members before the formal introduction to the rest of the troops. Linda didn't quite understand what he meant by *car*. Did he mean Betsy or Amy picking her up, she wasn't sure, but the butterflies in her stomach had increased every hour since she woke this morning. Looking at the clock, she hadn't needed to start getting ready for another hour, so she decided to sit down and do some knitting.

Over at the Thayer house, Candace had left about an hour ago to have her hair done and then a facial. Chip had just woken from a nap and decided to start getting ready. It was early, but at least he could get his shave and shower behind him. Standing in the bathroom, looking at himself in the mirror, he found his appearance had changed since his hospital stay. The long scar down the middle of his chest was the most noticeable change, but Chip felt that whatever was behind that scar had given him a new outlook on life. Looking at his face, the color was back, and he actually looked as fit now as he did before surgery. The one distinct difference he did notice was his eyes. To himself, he actually looked happy and at peace with himself, while before he saw an angry selfish person in the mirror. He said to himself, "This new heart has made me a different person. The fellow I inherited it from must have been a special person indeed."

As he continued to stare into the mirror, his mind drifted back. He was standing in front of this same mirror, getting ready to go into the office. He just returned home, after being gone all night.

He phoned Candace the previous evening around 9:00 p.m., telling her that he was going to check into a room. He said that he had too much to drink and didn't want to drive. Candace told him that it was a good idea, then hung up the phone. The drink had nothing to do with it; Chip, the ultimate cad, had gotten a room for him and the young woman he'd met at the bar just a few hours ago. Chip, looking at himself in the mirror with a sly grin, complemented himself. Candace wasn't home when he arrived, and he didn't give it a second thought about where she was, because he really didn't care.

Now coming back to his senses, he again looked at himself and said, "What a bastard I've been, to my wife, my daughters, and the people I work with. Enough is enough."

As he was in this state of revelation, Candace returned home, "Chip!" she yelled out.

He stuck his head out of the bathroom and yelled back, "Hey, sweetie, let me look at you!"

Candace walked over to the bathroom, and Chip smiled at her, "You look wonderful!"

Candace smiled and said, "Thank you, it's time to get ready, don't you think?"

Chip replied, "We have time. I know I'm a bit slow-moving, but not that slow. I'm so looking forward to tonight."

"So am I, Chip, this feels like a new beginning."

Chip then said, "It is, sweetie. I promise, it is."

# Chapter 43

It was now five twenty, and Linda looked at herself one final time in the mirror. She hardly recognized the woman in the reflection, with the new hairdo and makeup, again thanks to Candace's generosity. She began to wonder how much her life was going to change after tonight. Obviously, the new income will change her life immensely, but as much as the foundation was to be for charity, she didn't want to be a charitable case herself. She intended on earning this. One thing Linda realized was how cold the world is, with her entire life being a victim of such. Losing the only person that ever loved her had become almost too much to bear. The coworkers at the store were the only people to give her some type of normalcy, but when she put in her notice to leave, they all became instantly distant, which bothered her but at the same time didn't really surprise her. Outside work, she seldom spoke or spent any time with them.

The telephone rang, startling her. *Who could be calling?* she thought. Picking up the phone, and saying *hello*, the voice on the other end said, "Mrs. Shott, this is your driver. I'm down front, and I just wanted to let you know that I'm here."

She apologized, "I'm sorry, I'll be right down."

Linda hung up the phone, grabbed her coat, and headed out and down the steps to the outside. As she stepped out, she stopped in her tracks. There was a long black limousine with a man in a black suit and hat standing by the rear door waiting for her. "Oh my gosh," she said aloud, "this is for me?"

Smiling, the driver said, "Yes, ma'am," as he opened the car door for her. She anxiously walked to the car and got in.

The drive to the office was enjoyable. There was no conversation as she was being driven, but she felt as if she was floating on a cloud. The drive was too short, and she felt she could ride around in this car for days. Stopping in front of the building where the banquet was being held, the driver said, "Here we are, ma'am." As he started getting out of the car, he noticed that the woman he was driving started opening her door. "Please, ma'am," he said, "I'll get the door." With that, Linda stopped and waited for him. He helped her out of the car and wished her a good evening. Linda thanked him and entered the building.

# Chapter 44

As Linda entered the building, standing in the lobby were Chip, Candace, and the other members of the board, along with a personal assistant who came walking over to Linda with Chip and Candace following. The person approached Linda and said, "Ma'am, may I take your coat?"

Linda said, "Why, thank you."

He helped her take it off, then as he walked away, Chip came up to her and gave her a hug. "Are you ready for your big night?"

Before she could answer, Candace came over and said, "Linda, you look terrific!" The two women embraced.

Linda said, "I have to thank you again for everything."

"My pleasure," Candace replied. They walked Linda over to where the board members were congregating and drinking cocktails; introductions were made all around. All the board members were smiling and anxiously waiting to meet Linda personally.

As Linda looked around, she noticed that none of the other company employees were there. Before she could ask, Chip said, "Linda, this is the pre-prebanquet cocktail party. The others will be along in another thirty minutes or so. I wanted you to meet the board first, just to let you ease into this." He said with a chuckle, "My plan is to introduce you to the group as a whole at the conclusion of the award ceremony. Then afterward, there will be a couple of hours to mingle and meet everyone."

Linda just giggled, shrugged her shoulders, and said, "Okay, sounds pretty dramatic."

Chip, Candace, and the entire board laughed.

# Chapter 45

The award presentation ceremony was now in full swing. With the dinner and champagne behind them, Chip was at the podium calling up the award winners one at a time, giving a little complimentary word to each as he gave them their award. As he spoke about the final award of the evening, Candace, Amy, Betsy, and Linda were on the side of the dais, out of sight of the adoring audience. Chip then said, "Our final two awards of the evening, as it turns out, are being presented to the same person. This has never occurred in the forty-nine-year history of this company. The award for Rookie Salesperson of the Year and Company Salesperson of the Year goes to Trevor Alexander."

Trevor bounced up to the dais, received his award, and started to give an acceptance speech. Linda, who was nervous with her mind racing, did not hear a word of the speech. As he concluded, he waved to the applauding crowd then returned to his seat.

Chip raised his hands to quiet everyone, and he then began to speak. As he did, Candace turned to Linda, "Are you ready for this?"

Linda then exhaled and said, "I think so."

Candace then gave her a big hug, with Amy and Betsy following suit. "Oh, I almost forgot. Linda, Chip wanted me to give you this." With that, Candace handed Linda the silver half-dollar with the image of John F. Kennedy. She continued, "Chip thought this had brought him good luck during the surgery, and he now wanted you to have it for good luck."

Linda was stunned! She recognized the silver coin immediately but had forgotten about it during the entire ordeal Bo was going through. Linda was speechless. How did Chip come by this? As Chip continued to speak, she barely heard a word. Chip continued, "As you all know, I've been through quite an ordeal, as well as an awakening. When I went into the hospital, I knew I had an issue with my heart, but not knowing what it was. I thought the doctors knew the answer and would fix the problem, whatever it may be. What I've come to understand since is that not only was I a very ill person, but neither the doctors nor I knew that I was in need of a new heart. My heart was no longer functioning as a normal heart should. More so than a poorly functioning heart, what I was suffering from even more was a rotten heart. At the hospital, my wife and two daughters met a woman who was going through a terrible time, as her husband was not doing well. Through their conversation, my wife, Candace, realized that the relationship this couple had was something that many of us never experience. The love they had for each other was total, yet their possessions of not only material things but also outside friendships were few. Their entire lives, both were scorned by their peers, yet the two of them had a connection with each other that the rest of us never had. Yes, as a company, we've done very well. All of you in the audience tonight have achieved great success in the business world, but how many of us experienced the total love that these two have shared? I, for one, am jealous. (*choking up a bit*) I haven't been the greatest husband and father in the world. (*the audience now becoming surprised at his openness*) I've done things that I'm totally ashamed of, (pause, then *now starting to chuckle*) and I know I've not been the easiest guy to work for. (*With that, the audience started to laugh. After allowing the laughter to die down, he paused.*) The person I'm about to introduce to you is the most generous and sincere person I've ever had the honor to meet. It was she, while being informed that her husband would not recover from his terminal illness, that in fact, the love of her life would soon pass on, signed papers to allow them to transplant his heart into the chest of this shallow man (*pointing at himself, now Chip again started to become emotional, as his voice began to rise*). This new life that I've been blessed with will no longer be wasted! (*pointing to all those in the audience*) It was all of you who wanted to get involved in both community and charitable work, and it was this selfish bastard standing in front of you who squelched it at every turn. Not anymore! (*he paused and regained his composure, with his voice returning to normal volume*) So now, without further ado, I want to introduce you to the president and chief executive officer of the Robert and Linda Shott Foundation for the Underprivileged, Linda Schott."

Linda was holding and staring at the coin as Candace said, "Linda, Linda," and gave her a soft push toward the dais. Linda then somewhat sheepishly walked up to the podium with Chip giving her a long hug. She then turned to the audience, not sure of how to react. The people were all standing, applauding for her. Linda looked over the audience as they continued to applaud her. As she did, at the rear of the hall, Linda focused in on an aura. It was a faint image of Bo, who was also standing and applauding for her with the largest grin on his face. She saw no pain in his smile, and she then smiled back toward him. He then waived to her and blew her a kiss, then his image began to fade until it was gone. Linda then, for a brief moment with her smile subsiding, looked up to the heavens and thanked God then again turned to the audience, smiled, and mouthed the words "Thank you, thank you," several times.

*The end*

## About the Author

C.J. Herak was born in 1958 in Cleveland, Ohio. Raised in Euclid, Ohio, and graduated from Euclid Senior High School in 1976, he became a firefighter for the city of Euclid in 1984, and during his career, Chris also attended culinary school. He retired from firefighting in 2014. As his career as a firefighter was coming to a close, he became interested in theater and has been in twenty community theater productions to date.

The idea of this story was partially inspired by two of the author's acquaintances. This story evolved over a decade of working on and off, especially during the COVID-19 pandemic. After writing a play, Chris focused intently on finishing this story, which is his first fictional novel. Chris has been married to his wife Jayne for forty-two years, and they have two sons, Zach and Trevor, daughter-in-law Valerie and granddaughter Jillian.

Printed in the USA
CPSIA information can be obtained
at www.ICGtesting.com
LVHW040830190124
768648LV00036B/486